D1071823

THE MAN & WOMAN THING

ALSO BY GEORGE B. LEONARD

EDUCATION AND ECSTASY

THE MAN & WOMAN THING

AND OTHER PROVOCATIONS

by George B. Leonard

DELACORTE PRESS / N.Y.

Library of Congress Catalog Card Number: 79–108659
Manufactured in the United States of America
First Printing

ACKNOWLEDGMENTS

I especially want to thank Paul Fusco, who shared many of the labors that have found their way into this book, and Marshall McLuhan, who co-authored "The Future of Education" and "The Future of Sex." Members of my own family keep getting more important as sources of ideas, but are too numerous to cite here. I do want to offer my gratitude to Ross Claiborne, Price Cobbs, T George Harris, Richard Kennedy, Leo Litwak, Sterling Lord, Michael Murphy, and M. W. Sullivan; and to many good people at *Look* Magazine, including William Arthur, William Attwood, Martin Goldman, William Hopkins, Allen Hurlburt, and John Poppy—not to mention the remarkable woman to whom this volume is dedicated.

For PATRICIA CARBINE

CONTENTS

PART I

EYES IN THE DARKNESS

THEY burned this whole block down. . . . They burned this block. . . . They gutted this block. . . . They had tanks all over this street. . . . They burned down every pawn shop on 12th Street." We drove slowly through the silent early-summer darkness of Detroit. Our guide spoke evenly, matter-of-factly. That morning we had visited Cleveland slums. The next day it would be Chicago—then, on subsequent days, San Francisco–Oakland, Los Angeles, Atlanta and Washington. We were a group of journalists on a seven-day, seven-city tour of U.S. ghettos. Thirty years from a new millennium, we inscribed a sweeping circle around the face of a nation and found scars. Atlanta, my home town: a new stadium, civic center, arts center; a new skyline that might be said to reveal the energy, the enthusiasm and the values of this age and this people. Also a shadow self: slums. Our guide there seemed half out of his head. Words couldn't express his outrage. He opened his mouth but nothing came out; the right half of his face contorted until an eye was almost closed; his head bobbed from side to side as if receiving invisible blows from right and left. There was, you see, this . . . *injustice*. He drove with dogged fury. He had a list of 17 ghetto areas and would show us every one. Near the airport: unpainted shacks, sagging dirt roads, outhouses, no mail delivery. A freight train bumped heavily past; every freight car was loaded with three decks of shining new automobiles from the neighboring Ford plant. Our auto springs creaked as we porpoised over gulleys and shot out past the Carling Brewery toward the next ghetto. Six days of this kind of touring had exhausted us. The journalist who shared this guide and car with me wondered if we would have to see *all* 17. Our guide's head cocked to one side. He tried to answer, but nothing came out. He drove on furiously. (*Injustice!*) Rutted roads, rotting wood. Two young Negroes waiting to cross a street cursed our white faces. "What are you staring at? Go on home." We glimpsed a headline, something about the flight of Apollo 10. It seemed that once again we would successfully circumnavigate the moon. Our guide grunted. A front wheel had jammed in a deep rut and the back wheels spun until the ugly, acrid smell of burning rubber made us cough. At last we lurched out of our trap (during which interval Apollo 10 had glided effortlessly a thousand or so miles through space) and continued our tour. At the end, the odometer showed that we had traveled more than 100 miles, almost all of it within slums.

"Will there be riots?" I asked our guide.

"Not this summer maybe. People can't get together. But, maybe . . ." He smiled in, toward himself.

Suddenly, it seems, we have lost our way. We look around for comprehensible definitions of man and woman, for winnable wars, for racial peace. But there's no way of turning back. You can buy a car named Marauder with a red line stretching to 120 on the speedometer. But you won't be a marauder and the red line will measure only your impotence in heavy traffic. You can hock half our GNP for arms, but it won't buy you military glory. Barbed wire, gas and clubs no longer convince a man of his place.

Those old days were a lie. Self-deception stood guard between perceptions and horror. Racial peace was slavery. Military glory was flesh burning and marrow oozing from shattered bones. The manly march West was rape and the wanton destruction of cultures. It seemed simple and heroic, but always there were eyes in the darkness, the victims' eyes, wide open and waiting. No peace with injustice, only waiting.

Because things are getting better, we see how bad they are, and how much self-deception has cost us, victim and oppressor alike. The truth costs less: turmoil and pain and a chance for a beginning. The three stories that follow are about darkness and awakening.

A SOUTHERNER'S APPEAL

IN THIS TIME of tragedy and violent change, it is strange to be a Southerner away from home. It is like living an old bad dream all over again. Hardly a day passes without something happening that gives me a start, a small shock of recognition. I am no longer surprised at the sound of the word "nigger" pronounced with a hard "r." But I am dismayed to observe among my Yankee acquaintances the gradual shrinking away from reality that goes along with racial prejudice. I do not want them to suffer the affliction that many of us Southerners have spent lifetimes escaping. I want my friends in the North and West to know, to *feel* what it is like to live as a white man in a segregated society. For I have been there.

In 1963, I returned to my hometown, Atlanta, Georgia, and on a perfect Fourth of July day went swimming with a group of my kinfolk at Piedmont Park lake. This favorite haunt of my childhood had been recently desegregated; half the swimmers were white, the other half, Negro. In the 1930s, such a scene would have struck me as more unbelievable than science fiction. But the water was cool, the air, still; the sun burned softly in a high, pale blue sky. Gradually, the novelty of integration faded, and we became immersed in the pleasures of the summer day.

The only ominous element was the presence of a scattering of middle-aged, shirt-sleeved men and poorly dressed women standing around the water's edge. My brother explained that these were rabid segregationists, drawn there by a perverse curiosity. He called them "red-necks," a term that conjures up scorching-hot cotton fields, bitter poverty, ignorance and implacable racial hatred. Possibly one of them had a pistol or a crude bomb hidden on his person. But it was not violence we read on their faces, or hostility or even horror. It was something far more eerie, something that sent shudders up my spine. They were gripped by an almost hypnotic fascination. Their lips were drawn back, the hard lines in their faces somehow softened, eyelids narrowed, eyes glazed. They were not really *seeing,* yet they could not move their eyes from the dazzling sunlit images before them. Their bodies must have been numb, for they were absolutely rigid; they sat or stood for minutes at a time, motionless.

All of us, North and South, who would understand the phenomenon of racial prejudice must look into those eyes. I had seen their same expression, that same zombie-like posture, at a Ku Klux Klan meeting in 1961 while a grotesque pantomime about the horrors of interracial marriage unfolded on the stage of Atlanta's former Tower Theater. I had seen it on the face of a minister as he told me how happy and contented all the Negroes were in the Mississippi town where Mack Parker had been lynched. I had seen it in Little Rock and at Ole Miss, while men and women spun for me their fantasies of proud old Southern traditions undermined by Communist agitators from the

North. And I am beginning to see that expression on Northern and Western faces.

Take it as a symptom, a clue to the true nature of prejudice. Up to now, we have skirted the truth. National leaders and experts have analyzed segregation and racial prejudice as a sociological phenomenon, a political gambit, an economic lever. In limited ways, it is all of those things. But we have got to go a step farther. If we of the white race are to move effectively against the malady that cripples us, we must see it for what it is, and call it by its true name. Start with those glazed, unseeing eyes. What you are looking at is not a political, sociological or economic phenomenon. It is dangerous, self-destructive madness.

Madness is not always a painful affliction; often, it is an escape from pain. The worst pain may come from giving up those delusions of which madness is made. Few Negroes or whites have been willing or able to experience the pain of truth. One Negro author has made a start. In *The Fire Next Time,* James Baldwin took us near the heart of the Negro's side of the madness. He revealed the hatred, suspicion and suppressed anger most Negroes feel for almost all whites. He insisted that, if whites solved their own problems, there would be no Negro problem. He warned that, unless this nation ended its racial nightmare, it would perish.

Through Baldwin's words, thousands of white Northerners looked into the Negro heart for the first time, suffered the pain, then the relief, of tearing out their "liberal" racial delusions. ("Negroes are just like whites and are dying to enter the white world; all we have to do is contribute to the NAACP and invite at least one Negro to our cocktail parties.") Baldwin could tell only half the story.

He laid bare the dark secrets of Harlem streets and back rooms, but those secrets are not so dark as what is hidden in the racist's heart.

Men who would murder a fourteen-year-old boy because, possibly, he whistled at a white woman, or those who would set a bomb to explode during a Sunday-school service attended by little girls, have lost all touch with reality. But it is not enough to restate the obvious. We must look into the hearts of "reasonable," "moderate" men —those who live in governors' mansions or sit in the U.S. Congress; our friends, our relatives, ourselves.

The madness associated with segregation takes several forms; all involve the failure of perception, the inability to make sense from the information presented to the senses. We have no trouble "understanding" our servants or our friends' servants. As long as a Negro is a servant or a slave —that is to say, not a human being—we can face him. If we should confront him as a human like ourselves, however, we might feel what he feels, and that would be unbearable.

Almost every white Southerner must start from childhood building defenses against the danger of seeing the truth. He walls himself off from one emotion after the other; he draws the shades of his sensibilities. Because he lives in a deficient society, he is not aware of his deficiencies. But to be cured is overwhelming; one realizes then that hardly any aspect of the segregationist's personality has not been damaged. Almost every white Southerner starts out as an emotional, intellectual, visual, aesthetic cripple.

A few days after the Fourth of July, I drove from Atlanta to Monroe, Georgia, some 40 miles to the east. Stone

Mountain, just beyond Atlanta's outskirts, seemed reduced in scale. That huge, implacable outcropping of dark granite holds a mystic significance for the Ku Klux Klan. On many a dark night, hooded Klansmen have climbed its gently sloping west side to engage in secret ceremonies lighted only by the glare of flaming crosses. I knew nothing of this in my childhood. (My parents never spoke of the Klan, at least not in front of the children.) Still, the mountain had had a special magic for me during countless drives between Atlanta and Monroe, where my mother's people lived. Sitting in the back seat, my sister and I had always vied to be first to spot it, and then had become silent and a little awed as Route 78 took us up close, so that the mountain loomed over us, a lonely bulk by day, a heavy shadow against the stars at night.

Now, in a changing Georgia, even this had changed. Stone Mountain was being converted into a sort of Disneyland South. The cable tower and buildings on the mountaintop looked out of place. Stone Mountain was no longer lonely or magnificent.

But as I drove on eastward, the highway became familiar again. The little towns that had marked our progress toward Monroe—Snellville, Split Silk, Loganville, Between—still looked rundown and indolent. As in past summers, the raw red earth, the rolling pine forests, the fields of cotton and corn sweltered beneath a pulsating sky. The road was lightly traveled, and as I moved into the dreamlike world of childhood, the wheels of my rented convertible seemed hardly to touch the shimmering pavement.

On one deserted stretch of road, I stopped the car to feel again the suspenseful silence of the Southern countryside (a lone bobwhite calling across the cornfield, the distant hypnotic rise and fall of a cicada's song) and to smell the sweet, hot fragrance struck out of the earth by the sun. I realized then that no other part of the world would ever vibrate for me like this, and I realized, too, that I truly *loved* the South and always would. Beyond reason, beyond place or time, I would always love this lonely, tragic land whose people find it so hard to admit their own parts in our nation's darkest tragedy.

White Southerners need love perhaps more than anyone else. Northerners often cannot believe in "Southern hospitality," but it is real, and it can exist, *must* exist, side by side with slavery, suppression, police dogs and lynchings. The white minority in South Africa also has a reputation for personal hospitality. Both peoples are beset by a perpetual loneliness. In some far corner of their hearts, they know their treatment of their black brothers is immoral and inhuman. They sense, without conscious awareness, that they have had to block off some of their warmth and feeling in order to endure and perpetuate the system into which they were born. More than other people, they are driven to communicate warmly. They need to show others, and thereby reassure themselves, that they really are human and loving, that their system really is, somehow, not immoral.

Southern hospitality is real, but often takes grotesque shapes. Not long after the Ole Miss riots, Mississippi's Governor Ross Barnett was involved in an altercation with reporters in Chicago. One of his aides reportedly struck a photographer in the face. Barnett, according to *The Chicago Sun-Times,* "his teeth clenched, took several steps towards reporter Larry Weintraub and, shaking his fist in Weintraub's face, demanded, 'Give me those notes.' " The next day, he turned for a final word to another group of hostile reporters. With a broad, hospitable smile and in a sentimental tone of voice, he said, "Come to see us. Come by the Governor's mansion. . . . Yes sir, you come to the Capitol." This was no pose. It was precisely what would occur to a Southerner at such a moment.

Southern hospitality is the Southerner's desperate, pathetic outcry. He is saying, "I am not what you think I am. I am not what *I* think I am." The Southerner needs love, and in love (as some Southern writers have said) may come the final solution to the Negro problem. But ahead of that lies much pain for all of us, South and North.

During my early teens, I stayed three summers in Monroe, then a town of some 5,000. While my father commuted by car to Atlanta, my mother, sister, baby brothers and I shared the life of a typical mid-Georgia country town. Our summers revolved around my grandparents' spacious white house on Walton Street, on a different planet, it would seem, from Baldwin's Harlem. I had every reason to feel peaceful, protected and serene. My grandfather was one of Walton County's best-loved citizens. From 1931 until 1946, he almost always served in the Georgia House or Senate. As the county's only undertaker, he had prospered and won the respect of whites and Negroes for miles around. He was a farmer, too, operating several nearby farms with Negro tenant families.

Scenes from those long-ago summers came clearly back to me as I sat in my car beside the road near Monroe. More than anything else, I remembered the times my grandfather let me ride with him in his Chevy to one of the farms. We would start in the morning, before the heat of day had had a chance to weigh down upon the earth. We would drive past the icehouse and the silvery water tank at the edge of town and out into the country. After we turned off onto a dirt road, about three miles remained to go, and my grandfather traversed this distance at a majestic pace, hailing every soul we passed. "Howdy, Mose. . . . Howdy, Luke. . . ." They smiled. My grandfather smiled. The car smoothed out the bumps in the road. Field and forest rolled unevenly beneath an endless sky. The world seemed good.

I remembered those rides for the odors of the Southern earth: dew drying on dusty weeds; fresh manure; tasseled corn; and, most pungent and immediate of all, arsenic dust on a field of cotton. Long years later, even a hint of that smell would transport me back to Walton County countryside, and I would feel again the goodness of the earth and see the sympathetic, creased face of my grandfather next to me in the car, as relaxed and happy as he could be.

When we reached the mystic place on the road "where our land comes to," his eyes would grow narrow with pleasurable concern, and he would judge the progress of Marcus's plowing or dusting, or the growth of the crop. Then he would turn off to the right and mount the bumpy road that led up to Marcus's house.

Whatever was going on, ceased. The smaller children stopped their play and stood where they were, hands clasped behind them. The larger children stopped their chores in the barnyard, edged close; then they, too, stood still and mute. More small children slid like shy, curious beetles from the house, followed by Roberta, belly swollen in her shapeless dress, and they, too, stood still. Marcus smiled broadly, stocky and competent in overalls and crumpled hat. John, sleek and a head taller than his father, was expressionless. My grandfather got out and stood easy, hands on hips.

"Morning, Marcus."

"Morning, suh," he answered, hat in hand.

Both smiles were broad; the distance between the two men was appropriate and fixed.

"See you got the cotton weeded."

"Yessuh. Yessuh. Sho'ly did."

I always stayed in the car for a while. My eyes sought out the boy nearest my age, who was wearing my last year's shirt, and the little girl who was wearing my sister's dress of two years ago. The clothes were faded, and it made me somewhat uneasy to look at them.

"Sho' need some new plow harness."

"What you talking about, Marcus?" my grandfather said good-naturedly. "Your old lady keeps it patched up, doesn't she?"

Marcus paused. Though his face was fixed in an ingratiating smile, his eyes were cool and shrewd. He seemed never to look directly into my grandfather's eyes, and yet, like a gambler watching for a fifth ace, managed to keep a constant check on his expression. "Yessuh," he answered. "But she can't patch no more when ain't nothing there to patch on."

My grandfather laughed richly. He walked casually away from the house. Marcus and John followed. The dark figures in the yard began moving again, as they trudged away to hoe cotton.

I got out of the car and walked over to the barnyard. I looked into the chicken house and the barn, then climbed the barnyard fence to survey the surrounding fields. Somehow, I had always sensed that it would be wrong of me to go into the house itself; but since no one was near, I drifted over in that direction, leaned into the front door and quickly looked around.

Later, back in the car, I could visualize only fragments of what I had seen: pictures of Jesus nailed onto a warped, unfinished wall; a kerosene lantern; iron-framed double beds with mattresses that sagged almost to the floor; a rocking chair. But I had a powerful memory of the acrid, earthy odor that permeated the place.

"Their house is so little, and there are so many of them," I remarked about halfway back to town. "There isn't room for them."

"They've got the whole farm to stretch out in."

"But in the winter . . ."

"They keep each other warm." A knowledgeable smile moved over his face. "Why, you get all those pickaninnies in there, it's steaming warm."

"I know, but . . ."

"Listen, son, they don't know any other way of life. Why, they wouldn't *want* it any other way. They have plenty of food, and we certainly keep them in clothes. Don't you ever worry about those folks. They're a lot happier than any of us."

He drove on, occupied with his own thoughts.

"But what do they do at *night?*" I asked.

"At night? Why, they just sleep. When the sun goes down, they go to sleep, just like the birds. They sleep peaceful. None of us is ever going to be as happy as they are, I can tell you that. Life is simple for them. They know their place in the world, and they know their work. They're good, God-fearing people. Now, when a colored person goes to the city or gets out of his place or starts trying to be smarter than he is, then he'll be just as unhappy as . . . then he won't be happy anymore. But Marcus knows his place, and he knows his work. He's a good man, and I want you to know that I hold him in very high regard."

Again my grandfather withdrew into his thoughts. I started to ask another question, but something held me back. I had wanted to ask what they did *before* they went to sleep. There must, I thought, be a time like that. I had a vague yet powerful vision of all of them there in that small house, the sun down, the darkness gathering about them. Were they really so easily asleep? Didn't any of them lie awake for a while daydreaming or talking to each other? The car glided on toward town; fields and woods and farmhouses swept past me. I could smell the arsenic on the cotton fields, sharp and dizzying. I tried to imagine the Negro family lying in the darkened house, sleeping, breathing. But my thoughts blurred, and a feeling of strangeness came over me. There was something big and unexplained in my world, something I couldn't understand.

Strange things pop up at us like gargoyles when we are liberated from our delusions. Madness never seems so real as when we first escape it. My own liberation came through fortunate circumstances while I was still in my teens, even before I joined the Air Corps in 1942. When I first began meeting Negroes as equals, I thought I was entirely prepared, emotionally and intellectually. But at the beginning, something happened, so embarrassing to me I have never before been able to tell anyone. Each time I shook hands with a Negro, I felt an urge to wash my hands. Every rational impulse, all that I considered best in myself, struggled against this urge. But the hand that had touched the dark skin had a will of its own and would not be dissuaded from signaling it was unclean.

That is what I mean by madness. Because, from the day I was born, black hands had held me, bathed me, fed me, mixed dough for my biscuits. No thought *then* of uncleanliness or disease.

How can blacks and whites shake truth from the ancient web of lies in which they live? In 1963, a white Mississippi service-station attendant squirted water on a Negro who insisted on drinking from a white water fountain. The Negro drew a pistol and shot the white man dead. Horrible? Yes. A dreadful example to other Negroes? Yes. The Negro killed the white man and paid for it with a life sentence.

But there was truth in his action. He met the white man as an equal and let him know exactly what he was feeling about this one unbearable addition to a lifetime of small and large humiliations. Other Mississippi service-station operators, too emotionally crippled to feel what other people (Negroes) feel, will probably be able to read this simple message written in blood: "It is not necessarily perfectly OK and personally safe to squirt water on people just because they are Negroes." It is grotesque that whites and blacks must speak their true feelings with pain and death, instead of words. But that is one of the unavoidable consequences of relationships built entirely on lies. It is the flower and fruit of madness.

What did they do at night? That question began to haunt me during my boyhood summers in Monroe. In daylight, our docile darkies appeared at their appointed places, performed the tasks decreed by the white world;

then, when darkness fell, they went away, leaving white Monroe with hardly a trace of their passage. No sound from their houses reached Walton Street. Were they sleeping? The moon that shone into my sleepless room also shone in their windows. Did the moon make them restless, too? What happened when they got sick? Did they have doctors? Did their children have homework? Did they read the newspapers? There was really no way for me to know.

A half mile away, past trees and unplowed fields, most of the town's Negroes lived. I never had to be told that this was forbidden territory. Late one moonlit night, when we were bursting with excess energy, my sister, two friends of my own age and I ran for our bicycles, and, before we knew just what we were doing, all four of us were racing out of town on the dark blacktop road that ran past the Negro section. We kept going for three or four miles, pumping as hard as we could. Physically spent, we turned and started slowly back to town. We were aware now of our aloneness, and we became silent as we neared the houses clustered off to the right of the road. As we passed the Negro section, we could hear laughter, a baby wailing, dogs barking, radio music, someone (was it a man or a woman?) singing. I strained to hear words and see people. But the houses were too far away, and there were no street lights. Still, the windows glowed with the warm yellow of kerosene lamps, and the houses were unmistakably filled with wakeful life. Again a feeling of strangeness rose up inside me.

My sister gasped. I turned to see her bike swerve from a dark figure standing almost directly in our path. I swerved, too, gripped by terror. No word was spoken, and I could not make out the man's features, but he was looking at me very directly. He made no move toward any of us, and it was all over in a moment. But the inexplicable terror remained as we pumped quickly and quietly home; and I, never daring to look around, felt a tingling on the back of my neck until we were safe on Walton Street again.

Later that summer, I woke up one hot morning with the immediate knowledge that something awesome was happening. The phone had been ringing several times into my morning drowse, and when at last I came fully awake, I heard my mother ending a conversation: ". . . my feeling is, the less said about it, the better." I tried to get her to tell me what was going on. She answered in the generalities that are part of every Southerner's repertory. Her vague words were meant to reassure, but actually made me extremely uneasy. As soon as I could dress, I started downtown on my bicycle. On the way, I met my best friend, who was riding to get me. "That big buck nigger that raped a white woman—" he said with relish. "They're taking him into the courthouse today, and there's a crowd says they're gonna take him out of there. Let's get down to the square."

I felt a sudden stab of deep depression and then a strong desire to turn and go back to Walton Street. But I found myself pedaling alongside my friend past the Methodist church, toward the courthouse. For a moment, I thought of praying. I tried to think of God or the merciful Jesus of the Methodist Sunday school. What could Jesus do for the man they were after? For some reason, this seemed an improper question, and I was left with a sense of utter helplessness and futility.

The tree-shaded lawn before the old red-brick courthouse was filled with "country people." A few were carrying slabs of wood. Farm children were there, too, the smaller ones in their mothers' arms. The air was still beneath the trees, and everything was locked in a peculiar silence, broken only by commands from a state trooper.

My friend led the way, and as I followed him into the crowd, I had the feeling I could hardly breathe. I really did not want to go forward, but seemed to have no control over my motions. We worked our way almost up to the walk that led from the street to the courthouse steps.

All at once, a dull, inhuman sound rose all around me. Peering out between two farmers, I could see a state patrol car approaching: I glimpsed a dark head in the back seat. The strange sound, neither a roar nor a hiss, withered away in the hot, still air, and I felt heavy, insensitive bodies pressing forward against me. As the car pulled to the curb, I could get only intermittent glimpses of what was happening. The front doors were open. Two troopers got out and stood looking at the crowd. The back door opened. The crowd swayed forward. Troopers, arms outspread, pressed against the crowd, and I heard the trooper nearest me cursing under his breath. The press of bodies against me did not matter now; I was possessed with a compulsion to see the Negro, to look into his eyes.

My memory has him in chains, shackled to the two troopers in the back seat. Another dead sound rose from the crowd as the troopers dragged him from the car, and he struggled to find his feet. The crowd swayed forward again, and again a grotesque silence gripped the courtyard. In this silence, the troopers walked the Negro to the courthouse. As he passed only a few feet from me, he turned quickly one way, then the other, and it seemed his death-wide eyes met mine. But I knew he saw nothing. Fear had blinded him.

The crowd did not press forward again, and after the Negro had been in the courthouse for a while, some of the farmers started drifting away. My friend and I rode back to Walton Street without speaking. I went inside and lay on my bed, sick in body and spirit.

Something had happened to me when my eyes had met those of the Negro. *I had felt what he felt.*

The sickness left me, but it was days before my spirits rose. And there was another thing: never again could I believe what my elders said about Negroes. They did not sleep like babies. They never really slept. They spent their nights in passion and waiting and terror, their eyes white in the darkness. In the moonlight or during the blackest night, I felt their presence. They were not asleep.

It has taken many years and shouts from hundreds of thousands of Negro throats to convince white Southerners that their darkies have not been sleeping like babies. Many still do not admit it to themselves. Rather than believe that Negroes really want equality, these Southerners turn to any desperate rationalization. Many of them profess that the whole movement is the outcome of Communist agitation; right now, this explanation seems most acceptable and comforting. They would blame moon rays if they thought that story would stick. Give these deluded Southerners your sympathy; it is painful to be stripped of delusions.

And yet in every troubled spirit, there are two opposing forces. The segregationist clings to his delusion. He also wants to be rid of it and, in spite of the pain, he is relieved when it is gone. I was present at the historic night joint session of the Georgia legislature in January 1961, when

Governor Ernest Vandiver made a speech of surrender. He had campaigned with ringing declarations that he would not let a Negro in a white Georgia school. Many of the legislators present had earlier been utterly convinced that, when the moment came, they would gladly die to protect the Southern Way of Life. And yet here was their governor, not asking them to fight and die, not even asking them to close the state university, but the opposite: that they allow it to be kept open in spite of the registration of two Negro students. And what was the reaction of these men, most of them from small country towns not unlike Monroe? They filed out of the chamber silently, but their relief was as audible as a sigh. It was a painful moment, but they were glad to have it over with. One more of their delusions about themselves was gone.

The behavior of Southern politicians confuses many outside the South. When governors vow actions of defiance that obviously are impossible to carry out, intelligent observers conclude that they are being cynical, that they are speaking merely for political gain. Such would be the case if segregationists were like other people. They are not. They are seriously deluded men. They believe somehow that Negroes are pleased to be segregated, that everything would be all right if it were not for outside agitators, that they themselves truly plan to "stand in the schoolhouse door," to prevent integration even at the cost of their lives.

By failing to recognize the truth about segregationists, national leaders have miscued many times in the fight against segregation. Attorney General Robert F. Kennedy held a series of secret, long-distance telephone conversations with Mississippi's Governor Barnett just before the entry of Negro James Meredith safely into Ole Miss.

From beginning to end, Kennedy persisted in treating Barnett as an individual who meant what he said. Later, Kennedy realized he had made a mistake that might have led to an even greater tragedy than the riot of September 30, 1962. Looking back at the calls, and at Barnett's then and subsequent actions (see pages 55-63), one might judge that the Governor was not so much trying to deceive the Attorney General as he was confused about his own feelings and deluded as to what his own actions would be.

The lesson of Little Rock, Ole Miss, the Freedom Rides and Birmingham can be summed up in one sentence: He who deals with segregationists using reason and reason alone does so at his own risk. Rather, then, think of them as afflicted children who must be forced to walk: be sympathetic and kind, but be firm.

When I drove into Monroe at noon on that hot July day in 1963, much was the same. The Confederate monument, inscribed "Comrades," still stood guarding the courthouse square, and the old brick courthouse took me in an instant back to the summer days of childhood. Walton Street, too, seemed unchanged. The clear calls of the bluejay, the cardinal and the wren rang through the green haze of leaves that once had seemed to shut off the outside world. But there was a strange new silence. Most of my generation, I learned, had moved away, and now there were hardly any children on Walton Street. A new residential area had sprung up on the other side of town; the younger set, some of whom had migrated in with the town's new clothing plants, lived there, in houses almost as expensive and ordinary-looking as those to be found in any suburb of Atlanta or Los Angeles.

A way of life had passed away. The Negro tenant farmers had somehow disappeared. Many of the old farmhouses stood empty; the fields that once had bloomed with cotton now were planted with pines; the rabbit, the possum and the fox flourished. I learned that our old Marcus had died. His children, so far as anyone knew, had moved to the cities, mostly in the North.

Integration had not come to Monroe. But Atlanta now seemed closer, and the town's citizens knew that, sooner or later, "*they*" would arrive. There were bitter faces in Monroe, especially among the older generation. But there was also a sad sense of inevitability, a reluctant readiness for change, even a wish to have it all over with.

And, everywhere, I found lingering affection for my grandfather, who had died years earlier, followed within six months by my grandmother. He had lived a long life in the esteem of his fellows. He had always loved and had wanted very much to be loved. He had been as good as his society would allow. But I learned a sorrowful thing, and I discovered later that it is common throughout the South. He had not died peacefully. In the last months of his final illness, he had been haunted by terrifying hallucinations. Several men were "after him." He felt he needed a gun to protect himself. The men were Negroes.

I hate violence with a sort of revulsion that is more visceral than cerebral. Yet, when I first read of the Negro "riots" in Birmingham, my primary feeling was elation. From my childhood, I had known Birmingham as an oppressive, brutal, inhuman place. I was amazed that so many Negroes had had the guts to move so soon into its streets.

Uprisings can cause suffering, injury and death. But, for

Negroes, there is worse pain in a life of silence and submission. In the death of the spirit lies the ultimate human defeat. I know James Baldwin was wrong: the fire is not "next time." The fire was *then,* in the past, in the long years of so-called racial peace and harmony in the South, in the years when the madness of segregation burned the hearts and spirits of Negroes and whites alike. Each movement *away* from harmony built on lies is an escape from fire.

The truth can hurt. Not facing the truth can destroy. Face it: the Negro has grievances. They are real and pressing. Setting them right will cause pain and maladjustment in South and North alike. But pretending they are not real will not make them go away. Voting for George Wallace of Alabama will not make them go away. Waiting for everyone to be "ready" will not make them go away, but will only stiffen attitudes on both sides and increase the likelihood of violence.

Let a Southerner who loves the South and all its tortured people say a word to those responsible for upholding our nation's laws: Do not delay. Do not leave us with our madness. Hurry.

MEXICO: A DIFFERENT JOURNEY

GENERATIONS of novelists, poets and scholars have impaled themselves on Mexico's jagged contradictions. The experts savor their own bafflement. "We've been here twenty years," the Mexiphile couple informed us over a candlelit dinner in Mexico City, "and we only know that we know less about Mexico now than when we first came." The couple saluted each other with little nodding smiles of self-congratulation. "This mystery is *ours,*" their unspoken words seemed to say, "and don't *you* dare try to unravel it in two or three months."

Photographer Paul Fusco and I certainly weren't experts. We didn't speak the language and would have to work through interpreters. Even two or three *years* wouldn't be time enough to cover the entire country. And there was another thing: we were not alone. On the eve of the 1968 Olympics, journalists from around the world were turning their eyes to Mexico. Nearly every magazine we'd heard of was there. You have read some of the reports about the tasteful exuberance of the Olympics preparations, about a new generation of impatient and aware young people, about modern buildings and startling industrial growth, about the Cultural Olympics that brought writers, musicians and artists from many countries as counterpoint to the sports competition.

But we offer you a different journey. Paul and I, having no preconceptions, decided to follow our own impulses and reveal to you our own feelings. This is no well-balanced explanation of Mexico. It is subjective, a series of personal experiences—Paul's experience, for example, as he photographed the *penitentes* at Taxco:

> There are thousands of people carrying candles on the sides of the steep, narrow, winding streets. And no noise, almost complete silence. As the *penitentes* approach, you can hear the chains dragging on the sharp stones of the roads—a metallic *shunnk, shunnk.* You wonder what's happening. You have all sorts of mental side trips about people in dungeons. Then when the *flagelantes* approach, you hear a kind of soft *thunk.* They are hitting themselves on the back at a very slow, rhythmic pace—*thunk, thunk* —almost like a heartbeat. What's so strange is that you don't see any *response* to all this penance. Sometimes, when a particularly bad back comes by, some of the women draw away at what the person has done to himself. But there are no outcries, no moaning and groaning. Just silence. It's surreal, almost like a dream, where no one can talk. Everybody has a thing to do, and he just does it.
>
> It was very hot during Holy Week. During the day, heat falls on you like concrete. Even after dark, it's sweaty. Very late one night, I knelt behind this guy to get as close as I could. As I hunched down, I could feel a warm sensation on my face. I couldn't tell what it was until I rubbed my hand over my forehead, and then I saw streaks of blood on my fingertips. I was shocked to think there was human blood being sprayed on me, that this guy was doing such damage to himself. My first impulse was to turn away, even though I didn't. I felt I was violating him

by being so close. It was such a personal act that no one should be so intimate with it. But everyone seemed to accept me as part of it. The whole thing was *accepting*. This guy does this. That guy does that. Thousands come to watch. Everyone I talked with says it gets bigger every year.

But acts that shock the North American may seem commonplace to the Mexican. As the Mexican poet, Octavio Paz, has written,

> One of the most notable traits of the Mexican's character is his willingness to contemplate horror; he is even familiar and complacent in his dealings with it. The bloody Christs in our village churches, the macabre humor in some of our newspaper headlines, our wakes, the custom of eating skull-shaped cakes and candies on the Day of the Dead, are habits inherited from the Indians and the Spaniards and are now an inseparable part of our being.

The macabre images at Taxco may have been extreme, but they kept recurring in different guises as we wandered through Mexico. We spent a morning with the great muralist, seventy-two-year-old David Alfaro Siqueiros, in Cuernavaca as workmen and artists hurried to complete his *magnum opus* in time for the Olympics. Outrageous even in scale, the mural will depict the evolution of man and will cover the interior walls and ceiling of an auditorium two-thirds as big as a football field. In swirling, turbulent colors, giant figures seem always to be pressing into a storm. Again and again, throughout the mural's 4,600 square meters, one is brought up short with images of struggle, suffering and death.

There is a grand scale, an almost desperate boldness

about all things Mexican. The occasional abundance that bursts from the sun-blasted earth may be piled up in extravagant marketplace displays. Even death seems extravagant. Vultures dominate the sky and find honored roosts near the centers of villages. Dead animals dot the roadsides. Funerals become fiestas, and fiestas often are dedicated to the dead. Even schoolchildren, in their stories and fetes, learn that death is a casual companion, not a distant, improbable stranger.

In the bullring, death becomes an art form. The matador's sword, the aficionados would have us believe, strikes through the pasteboard wrappings of outer appearance to the hidden heart of the ultimate reality within. Existence is tragic; death is near. Fear and courage vie on a stage made bright and pure with color and ritual. But all of this is literary. My perceptions of *la fiesta brava* are swayed by too much reading of Hemingway and García Lorca and Barnaby Conrad. Paul Fusco came to the Fair of San Marcos at Aguascalientes in Mexico's high north country with fresh perceptions. He saw and felt for the bulls:

> La Punta is probably the biggest and most famous bull ranch in Mexico. The owner, Francisco Madrazo, showed me around. The sun was hot and sharp. There was no moisture in the air. Late in the afternoon, near sunset, we went to an enclosed area about the size of a football field where they kept the young bulls, two or two and a half years old. It was a place where they could stay and play and jump around and romp. They were great animals to watch, like a bunch of teenage boys. They were so busy, constantly moving, constantly butting each other. There was no malice in them. They were like exuberant kids who had to use up all the energy that was in them. They

weren't being bad. They were having a good time, and they enjoyed being there.

But something was missing. There were no girls. They kept looking for something—always jumping up on each other—but they didn't know what they were looking for. They wouldn't give up.

I couldn't believe these animals would do something cruel in the nature of arbitrary violence. Even the big ones out on the ranch—they looked very sullen and very strong, but didn't look like they would go up to something and be cruel, you know.

At the bullring, Francisco said he felt nervous. He said, "I want the bulls to perform well, but since they're *bulls,* you never know." I was very anxious myself. To see all that force loosed in the ring is awesome. And I kept getting a lot of warnings that a bull might jump the wall into the protected area where I'd be shooting, and I wondered if I could get out of the way with all this camera junk around my neck. When the first bull came charging out —I knew he was coming; but it was still a surprise to see him there with all that immediacy—black, but dusty and shiny at the same time.

He runs out with a pounding of hooves on the floor of the earth, stops short, tosses his head and looks around to see where he is. He's come from a small pen, and now he's free, but he's not really free, and he's come to a place that has no meaning for him. You can feel the confusion on his part, with all the people yelling and screaming. It's a world in contrast to everything he's ever known—the freedom of the ranch, the big open sky, the acres of land. And now he's here. More quickly than I anticipate, there are men in the ring with the matador, tossing big capes around. And the bull charges. Nothing happens. Nothing is there. You can feel his perplexity. Then there are the men with these short-barbed wands with colored tassels and then the horsemen with the big spears, all jabbing into the bull's shoulders; then the matador working with the small cape. And then, at a certain point, the bull just gives up. He's been thrusting, thrusting, with no results, and he decides, "This is a bad place to be." It's just at that point that the matador comes in with a sword to kill him. The bull is just standing there, confused. The matador stands with his sword raised. Then, with one great burst of energy, he plunges the sword into the bull.

Right after that is the bad part. The bull stands there with his mouth open in a look of complete disbelief and unknowingness, and you can sense the life leaving his body. He kind of staggers, walks back a bit, and his legs give out from under him. He falls hard, straight down. It's not graceful or soft, but hard—*bang*—right down on the ground.

While the matador is taking his acclaim from the people, these two men come out running with two donkeys and in an *instant* throw a chain around the bull's horns. They send the donkeys flying back toward the exit, and the bull is like a boat, spraying a wake of sand behind him.

Acapulco is *not* Mexico, the Old Mexico Hands told us sternly. This was only one of many places—all of them popular with tourists—that had been designated for us as "not Mexico." We were almost ashamed to admit we were going there.

We loved it.

The service was sometimes as sloppy and rude as we'd been told to expect. The American tourists were sometimes as arrogant as we'd been led to believe they would be. The electricity at our hotel failed almost daily. But then, the service was often quick and polite, the visitors, gracious and happy. And the unexpected failure of man-made power only sharpened our awe of the power falling from the sky, both day and night.

There is something fluid about Acapulco. The air is humid, rich and thick; it offers one the illusion of living sensuously under water. Anyone who stubbornly refuses these delights, it seemed to us, must be somehow out of touch with his body and senses. The human body in all its glory is indeed hard to ignore in Acapulco. Every female with a figure for it and some without wear bikinis. This costume is sanctioned for all but the most formal occasions. Vacationing schoolteachers from Chicago sit in bikinis and false eyelashes at the circular La Isla bar at the Acapulco Hilton. A bikinied housewife selects postcards in the lobby to send her children in Harlingen, Texas. Minor-league jet-setters float in the pool (with underwater barstools) at the Villa Vera. And along the edge of the beach, "afternoon nightclubs" provide shabby jazz, cha-cha and rock for bikinied patrons who dance stickily, lap up Margaritas and arrange rendezvous for later in the day, the night or the early morning.

We learned that Acapulco is best enjoyed by those who can flow with the current, unabashedly seeking thrills—parachuting behind a speedboat, game fishing, skin diving, water skiing, body surfing or just soaking up energy from the sun. Here is no harsh land. The poverty and suffering all around will stay up in the hills a while longer, one hopes.

But Acapulco *is* Mexico. And those *are* Mexicans waiting on the edges of our fun-filled days. What is that expression on their faces? We cannot tell. It is a mask. This mask is real, not just a figment of our naïve imaginations; bemusing to expert as well as newcomer.

> The Mexican [writes Octavio Paz] seems to me to be a person who shuts himself away to protect himself; his face

> is a mask and so is his smile. In his harsh solitude, which is both barbed and courteous, everything serves him as a defense: silence and words, politeness and disdain, irony and resignation. . . . He builds a wall of indifference and remoteness between reality and himself, a wall that is no less impenetrable for being invisible. The Mexican is always remote, from the world and from other people. And also from himself.

We were bewildered. Words would say one thing, while faces were saying something quite different. We sought out fiestas, always searching for the ecstatic moment when the Mexican would burst forth from his mask and explode in a revelation of true feelings. The fireworks exploded, the colors exploded, the music exploded, the words exploded. The faces remained strangely sorrowful and alone. During the fair at Aguascalientes, a man who had hired a mariachi band for himself insisted that the band serenade Paul. Again and again, he embraced Paul and said, with a sort of desperation: "We are all the same, señor. We are having so much fun." His face said something else.

In Acapulco, we chartered a boat, a Toonerville Trolley version of an oceangoing yacht, and worked our way up the coast to Zihuatanejo. There we found the sparkling beach and bay, the incredibly clear water we'd been promised. We also found, in the village, some more of those improbable sights that bemuse, appall and, finally, perversely delight visitors to Mexico: three village girls gleefully racing and whipping their leashed piglets; a man inexplicably dragging a dead dog through the main streets of town.

On the way to Zihuatanejo, we went ashore at a tiny fishing village. It was late afternoon; the setting sun poured garish orange light on three pool tables under a flimsy thatched roof. A horde of men swarmed around the tables, playing the maddest games of pool I'd ever seen. They pitched money back and forth, repeatedly shot the cue ball off the tables, and never paused in manic motions that had the quality of old movies. We knew these men would be going out to sea that night in tiny boats to fish for red snapper. When we resumed our cruise after dark, we saw their brightly pulsing lamps farther out to sea than we were, very brave, very poignant, beneath heavy black clouds.

Later we journeyed to the Oaxaca Valley, searching for a simple, isolated village where men, women and children would be dealing with the ancient equations between soil and sun, water and drought, life and death. At last, high up a winding mountain road, we found San Lorenzo Albarradas. In a sense, it is a model village. It has no electricity and only the vestige of a road. But its 1,255 people are proud of a new diesel-powered water system (with communal water spigots scattered around the village) and a four-room elementary school. During our stay in San Lorenzo, it was the school and the children we kept coming back to.

The children were beautiful. There was something dark and deep and yet unexpectedly radiant in their eyes: perhaps a sense—we would call it a tragic sense—of place and of timelessness. They would go through six years of schooling. They would not likely go on to the world beyond. They would spend all their days in San Lorenzo, bounded by hilly fields and dry valleys beneath an enormous sky. They would look to the sky for their fortune; the rains would come or would not come. They would get married and have children. They would plow fields or weave straw mats. Even now, they watched wordlessly as girls only a year or two out of school walked by carrying their new babies.

And they know death very well. At a school pageant performed for us, the only players never to change costumes were Death and The Devil; there was a part for them in every act. When a San Lorenzo woman died unexpectedly in her early fifties, it was accepted as nothing out of the ordinary. Men gave out cigarettes and mescal liquor. Women baked tortillas for the guests. The bereaved husband got very drunk. The dead woman lay on the earthen floor of her house like one sleeping in soft candlelight, with a crown of flowers on her head. The children continued playing.

Yet there was victory in the very simplicity of village life. Paul and I finally found our moment of joy and transcendence, as you will see later, in something as commonplace as a man loading charcoal into a truck.

But that isn't quite right, for nothing is really commonplace in Mexico. Everything in this strange country is *strange,* to Mexican as well as to foreigner, and there is some little twist to the most "ordinary" event.

Even the Mexican past holds no sure clues (though the precipitous mixing of Spanish with Aztec cultures was bound to create the unexpected). Paul and I visited archaeological sites with other tourists. We traveled to the spooky Mayan ruins in the jungles of Palenque and to those high, regal Zapotec ruins at Monte Albán, near Oaxaca. We heard how the Indians often deserted the most elaborate, beautifully constructed sites; no one knows why. Most of the Indian records were destroyed by the Spanish conquerors. The archaeologists we interviewed had more questions than answers.

The mystery is the essence and the appeal. Groping for words to describe what draws them to Mexico again and again, American tourists usually end up saying, "It's more *foreign* than anything in Europe, and it's right here."

To us, Mexico seemed not only "foreign" but almost completely unpredictable. The absence of order in the European or American sense is what exasperates. It is also what delights and rejuvenates. In our orderly, antiseptic culture, everything in life tends to fall into place. Man is a pattern-recognizing, pattern-creating creature, and he sometimes patterns too well. Every job, every marriage, every significant human relationship moves toward routine. A familiar word or act in our lives is likely to trigger a time-worn scenario that will differ from previous versions only in details.

Such scenarios are nearly impossible in Mexico. Something unexpected, improbable, unfathomable is almost certain to shatter the routine. The Mexican—as "inscrutable" as an Oriental and yet as excitable as a Latin—is never very sure himself what he is going to do next. British writer John Lincoln, among others, describes occurrences that boggle the sensibilities and leave one laughing or sobbing: his difficulties in getting a dead man removed from the side of the street in front of his house; his flight in an airliner that suddenly heads in the wrong direction and lands to pick up a drunken mariachi band.

Eventually, all the airlines will run in the right direction. There will be a "new Mexico," with order and prosperity; it is, in fact, already much in evidence, even though we have not treated it in this story. As we ended our trip, we couldn't help hoping that this new Mexico—while ending poverty and psychic isolation—would retain the rich depths of the old. Some of our knowledgeable informants in Mexico City seemed to envisage *their* new Mexico as a sort of extension of Lincoln Center. "Do you know," we were asked, "what records they play at our youth center? *Beethoven!*" We were told again and again about the series of lectures by playwright Arthur Miller. We were reminded that such sculptors as Alexander Calder were contributing giant works to the Olympics.

Beethoven, Miller and Calder are all very fine, but it seemed to us that Mexico—with its richness, its strangeness and its raw power—could do better by remaining unique. The land itself—curving off the bottom of the North American continent like an angry tornado—constitutes a stage for high drama. And the people have a theatrical sense that needs no prompting by foreign playwrights. We saw this theatrical sense in all segments of the population—in intellectuals and artists, taxi drivers and waiters. But we most treasured it in the simple villagers we came to know. It was they who, at last, opened their hearts and revealed their true feelings. We remembered that simple, "ordinary" moment in the woods above San Lorenzo. Here is how Paul Fusco described it in a letter to his wife:

> The sky over Oaxaca was filled today with about a hundred different kinds of clouds. They have clouds I've never seen before. As we climbed the hills and mountains leading to San Lorenzo, the tops of other mountains ducked and appeared again from behind clouds, vapor, mists and rain. A man was ploughing with oxen on a rounded field on a knoll under this magnificent sky in incredibly beautiful light. We stopped to watch. A companion followed after him planting corn in the rows, one kernel at a time, and burying it with his foot. It is impossible to describe the vastness of nature hovering over these two men and their

oxen. They are like infinitely brave men who dare to suppose they can somehow gain some benefit by working against that immense nature.

Take one man working out in the woods where they were making charcoal in a cave. Take a burlap bag of charcoal five feet high and almost three feet across and fill it until it weighs 200 pounds. This man was a little shorter than I and his arms only slightly larger than mine. Seven men work together loading the bags of charcoal, and they keep telling us to wait and watch this guy carry a bag. I figured that all the men would band together to load the truck and that just for pictures this one guy would lift one bag for me.

They place a plank on a 30-degree angle from the truck to the ground. Men put small hooks into the cloth of the bag and laugh. "All is ready." Two men go to the bag. The single man bends over like a football lineman, legs widespread, back parallel to the ground, head tucked into his chest. And he slams his spine and shoulder into the side of the bag one foot above the ground. They all heave and the bag comes up above the ground in an arc and he is upright with 200 pounds of charcoal high on his shoulders. He turns and takes small steps to the board and climbs up–zip–and heaves the charcoal into the floor of the truck. Everyone laughs and cheers: "He did it!" He comes back down and to my great surprise assaults another bag, then another and another and loads all 14 by himself. And he always does. Six men stand around while he is loading the truck. "He is the only one who can do it," they say, and he laughs all the while, even while the fibers of his body burst beneath the brown sweat-shiny skin. Ligaments leap out of his neck like steel cords as he plunges at the bags like a bull tossing a horse, neck and head low, sweeping up the bags high over his head. After he loads the truck he stands and smiles at me. Everyone is laughing and feeling very good because I have seen it. That's true. I have, but I still don't believe it and even less understand it. They all could have joined together to lift the bags into the truck as a team, but no, "He is the only one who can do it."

I must be grateful to the people of San Lorenzo, because they gave me their hearts, especially those seven men loading charcoal. Some kind of male, effusive joy pervaded all of their work and talk. It is hard work. They spoke openly of the poor wages and the hard, trying life in San Lorenzo. But somehow they never breathe defeat or malice or malevolence. They seem to say, "Yes, life is hard and offers little. We work hard. We eat and sleep and have families. We will never be better off than we are now. Let's hope we won't be any worse off, but,—well, life is to live." Maybe it's the Zapotec in them. Maybe there is a strength that comes from living on and under a scope of nature so huge and overpowering it catches your breath. Maybe it's the knowledge that because they can almost win against that giant hovering over them they are really superman—really, really superman—because, "By God, we are still alive and can laugh together when we go out to face the odds against us. We are small men but, *ahhh,* our fibers are tough, our determination indomitable and, by God, if you take one of us in death, why, we will just have another child and go at you again." HOORAY FOR THE CHARCOAL MEN.

I guess the best way to end the trip is with the people of San Lorenzo. They are a hope that lives, how I cannot understand, under a tyranny of nature that's so cruel, so ravaging, so brutal—nature at its most severe and perverse. They are still up there, perhaps forever, on the mountain, willing and ready to take it all on, ready to carry whatever burden befalls them. They have prevailed and have prevailed to a soaring height, for they are alive and they can laugh.

LILLIAN SMITH'S LAST INTERVIEW

THIRTEEN YEARS AGO, Lillian Smith found out she had cancer. After surgery and two weeks' rest, she went back to her writing. Two years and two books later, the cancer returned, and she was told she could not get well. She did not believe it. She went on writing, traveling, teaching, driven, as always, to the most outrageous and bewildering of human acts, which is saying the simple, obvious truth before people are ready to hear it. The cancer came back again and again, eating away at the most vulnerable parts of her small, slim body. As the body wasted, the spirit grew.

She had enemies, white Southerners who feared her for seeing Negroes as people. They burned her house, a mountaintop retreat near Clayton, Georgia, destroying all her manuscripts, letters, mementos and pictures. But they did not defeat her. She moved to another house on the mountain and went on writing. There were other enemies, literate men in the South and North, who did something more hurtful than burning a house: they refused to comprehend her. Back in 1944, she had published *Strange Fruit,* a novel about an interracial love affair that had shocked the South and made her the darling of critics who thought themselves liberal on race. Some of these critics kept expecting another *Strange Fruit,* and when it did not come (her spirit grew; her writing encompassed not just race but all of humankind), they simply interpreted each new book in terms of their earlier favorite. To them, Lillian Smith would always be "that little lady in Georgia who wants to help the Negroes," and nothing more. They had their neat little box for her, and they tried to slap her down whenever she seemed to be escaping it. The stubborn incomprehension of these critics started to make her bitter, and sometimes, when she spent too many months on her mountain alone all day with nothing but her pain to focus on, she had to fight the bitterness as hard as she fought the cancer. But none of this could defeat her. She went on writing (at times with blood pressure as low as 50) and speaking the truth, explicit and unrelenting, no matter whether her words made enemies or friends.

Now it was the summer of 1966, and she lay gravely ill in Emory University Hospital in Atlanta while Negroes rioted in overheated Northern city streets. And once again her words had startled the nation from South to North: Lillian Smith, bravest white champion of Negro rights, had resigned from the Congress of Racial Equality to protest its rejection of nonviolence.

When I entered her hospital room, she held out both hands for mine. "I'm sorry I've kept you so long," she said, with the smile of an old fighter who knows precisely how badly the fight is going. I took her hands and told her the few days I'd spent waiting for her to be well enough to see me had given me a chance to read *Killers of the Dream* for the first time. "It's a work of genius," I said without exaggeration, for I had discovered in that neglected and misunderstood book an angry, severe, yet beautiful explication of the hidden causes of Southern racism, the deep roots of shame and pride, sexual repression and self-deception that brought madness up out of the Southern earth. In it, as far back as 1949, Lillian Smith had said the unsayable words that many of us, including myself, had only got around to wrestling with more than a decade later.

Dark eyes shone from a face that gave off a white aura, not of sickness but of an almost supernatural intensity, an impatience with unessential matters. The room was light and neat, and it contained none of the paraphernalia of mortal illness. "I'm a bit weak from lack of nourishment," she told me, after she had excused the friend who was staying with her and I had taken a chair. "They are feeding me intravenously, but I told them to take all the needles out while you're here. I also told them to leave us alone. Now, I'm going to get a little clinical for a moment. This new drug they're trying on me has the strange quality of making me look well. See my face?"

"Yes, you look very good."

"The drug works on my enzymes. It shakes me. If it works. . . . But this cancer—it's my ninth flare-up—it seems to be telling me that it means business. This may be my last interview."

I had phoned Miss Smith shortly after her resignation from CORE, and she had told me to come on to Atlanta. Since we knew and understood each other, she had said, we wouldn't have to waste time establishing contact. And she did want to make sure that her resignation wouldn't be misunderstood. "My telegram to CORE is a good expression of what I feel," she had told me on the phone. "It criticized the whites as much as it did CORE, but the news stories left out a lot of that part." She had sent the wire to CORE director Floyd McKissick and it read, in full, as follows:

> I strongly protest the dangerous and unwise position CORE has taken on the use of violence in effecting racial change. I am therefore resigning from your advisory committee.
>
> For many years, CORE was firm in its belief in the use of nonviolence and refused tactics dictated by anger and hate. Its leaders believed that only love and compassion, reason and a vigilant search for truth could bring about creative human relationships. Unfortunately the stubbornness and dishonest methods of segregationists, the violence of the Klan and the blind complacency of many white church people have made it easy for the haters to take over from the more wise and patient leadership.
>
> Now we have new killers of the dream.
>
> CORE has been infiltrated by adventurers and nihilists, black nationalists and plain old-fashioned haters who have finally taken over.
>
> But the whites must carry much of the moral burden for this having occurred. White Americans have not met the creative Negro leadership halfway. They demand that Negroes show more wisdom and patience than they themselves show.
>
> CORE was pushed hard by the inertia and violence of many white Americans before its wise leadership succumbed. But I do not believe in the use of violence, however great the temptation.
>
> We are working for something bigger than civil rights; we are working for better human beings, we are working for excellence in our cultural life. How can we achieve these goals unless all of us meet this challenge with honesty and intelligence and good will and speed?

Now we spoke of the telegram, and I asked her if the new rejection of nonviolence among many Negroes and the rise of the "Black Power" concept had surprised her. "No," she answered, "I feared it from the beginning. I was in India in 1946, just as Nehru was starting to take over a little piece of the mantle of Gandhi, and already that beautiful movement was dragging itself in the mud of jealousies, power, pettiness. I was there for six months again in 1954–55, saw Nehru and spent much time with his family. They talked quite frankly to me about the petty jealousies in something that should have been beautiful.

"Later, back in the States, I thought of this when I made a speech commemorating the first anniversary of SNCC. I chose as my title 'Buying a New World with Old Confederate Bills.' I was reminding them even then of the problems they might have in the future. I said that after the Civil War—from 1865 on—America and England and Europe tried to buy the world of Africa and Asia with old Confederate bills—that is, with the belief that the white man's prestige was worth something. It wasn't.

"So I went on to remind the young men and women of SNCC how many good people had stood by them, and I told them I would choose to be their first critic. I said, 'You're going to have the same temptation that Jesus and Gandhi had—the temptation of personal political power. You will want to get power in your own hands, to manipulate, to use your kind of old Confederate money. You will want to stir people's hatreds.' I warned them about all of this.

"At the end of my talk, John Lewis [then chairman of SNCC] came up to shake my hand. His hands were ringing wet, and he said, 'I had the strangest feeling when you were talking.' I said, 'If you had that feeling, you really didn't need my warning.' John Lewis is a bright and good person, and now he's out of SNCC. Or has he come back since I've been here in the hospital?"

"No," I said, "he's still out of power."

She shook her head. "I feared it would happen. Now Black Power will last until white people and black come together and say the only power that counts is human power."

She gave firm emphasis to these words, lifting her head somewhat painfully from the pillow, and I thought of a summer's afternoon I had spent with her just a year earlier at her mountain retreat. I had come to interview her for a *Look* issue on the South, but before the afternoon was over, she had moved far beyond "the South" or "race" to sketch luminous outlines of man's future, of a new human power that was becoming possible on this planet. Though weak from her illness even then, she spoke with tightly focused energy and conviction, delicately balancing her immediate concern about the ongoing racial struggle against her larger vision that could give the struggle meaning and direction.

We ended up sitting on the floor of her bedroom, going through boxes of research material, surrounded by papers and books on Persian history, medieval heresies, evolution, modern science and—most central to her thought—the works of the Jesuit philosopher-scientist Teilhard de Chardin. Totally absorbed, I did not realize until I smelled a subtle change in the thin, piney mountain air that it had started raining quite hard outside, for the air was utterly still and the rain was whispering down through needles and boughs. In the green and rainy light, Lillian Smith's pain-ravaged face, circled around by curly white hair, was radiant with the hope that has grappled with suffering and disappointment and has prevailed.

Segregation (to summarize Miss Smith's view) is a strange but significant form of dehumanization. It is a striking example of mankind's most disastrous sin, the dualistic approach to life that separates body from spirit, dark from light, action from thought. By solving our race problem, we can show the way toward repairing all the chasms that split the world. But this we cannot do unless we see segregation not simply as something that concerns race but as an act, a defense, perhaps a ritual, that can be used in numberless ways. We can segregate ourselves from each other, from our own true selves, from God, from an idea, from art, music, science. The American South, for example, segregated itself from the richness of a great part of the last 3,000 years and thus became a culturally deprived region that is only now reawakening to the joys and opportunities of the present.

The worst thing about segregation is that it stops the human race from evolving. We started to evolve as human beings perhaps a half million, perhaps a hundred thousand years ago, when individuals came closer together, used each other as mirrors, began reflecting, *thinking*. Because they were so near each other, their minds blazed from proximity. As Teilhard de Chardin said, the mental temperature shot up. Because the world is round, Teilhard pointed out, men cannot escape each other, but must always move closer. As they rub their minds together, they become keener, brighter, more curious, more *human*.

Today, in the chaos of a fast-changing world, many people are behaving like children who are upset because they cannot run away from a world that is round. Some want to escape human growth by jumping off into outer space. Some want to run backward into the past. Some turn to violence. Some try to withdraw into ideologies, abstract schemes that often become, to their believers, more important than living human beings.

But we cannot escape each other, cannot remain segregated. Just as the nineteenth century was the age of ideologies and segregation, the twentieth century is becoming the age of human relations. Again, the mental temperature is shooting up. Suddenly, we are only a few hours from everyone on earth. Men in small groups, collaborating, can solve problems in a few months or weeks or even days that one man, working alone and in isolation, could never have solved had he lived a thousand years. At the same time, modern science is giving us the instruments and the insights with which to examine and understand ourselves so that we may open our hearts and minds to others. "It has crept upon us so quietly," Lillian Smith wrote in *The Journey,* "we have hardly noticed. But it is one of the significant events of the twentieth century: these groups of men and women, finding their tongues, sloughing off the old mutism and doing it just as science gives them the means of worldwide communication. Not arguing, not debating, not defending and entrenching their past mistakes. Not on trial. Simply saying, 'It was this way with me.' "

She went on to write about ending the subtle segregations within us: "Now, for the first time, we are beginning to bring together the fragments: to bind childhood to the rest of our life so that our reason can control it and thus reduce the anxiety which dictators, inside and outside us, exploit so lushly; to tie body to mind to feelings to fantasies to belief; to relate these to the rest of mankind and to the world; to relate power to humility, and responsibility to honor and freedom; to keep tenderness and truth close together."

Lillian Smith believes that we must end racial segregation to make ourselves and our world whole again. To end racial segregation, however, we must, *at the same time,* start breaking down all the other barriers that segregate our lives. We can and must change ourselves, not just superficially but down to the second and third layers. We can and must evolve into different and better human beings, not by withdrawing into ourselves but by forcing ourselves right out into the crowd, by working with and changing the institutions—government, church, business, school—whose sole purpose should be to make each of us more human.

Against this vision of infinite and ever-evolving human power, it is easy to see why Lillian Smith had to protest a policy that would build new walls between black and white just as it seemed to her the old walls were beginning to crumble. *Black Power.* No matter how great the provocation that created it, or the immediate satisfactions and gains, Black Power eventually works against the human power that builds lifesaving bridges between all races, all people.

In an Atlanta hospital room, at a time when Negroes and whites taunted and cursed each other on city streets, when innocent children suffered the pain of ignorant bullets, Lillian Smith and I talked about building new bridges. "Just as segregation is easy to define," she said, "integration is impossible to define. The new human relations offer us infinite options, the options of spiritual freedom. This means not that we'll be free to do what we *want* but free to do what's *right*. Eventually, the two will be one."

Again she lifted her head: "This idea of human evolution is so exciting. It's as if God is saying to us, 'You've been a baby long enough. Now grow up. I don't have to give you childish things like miracles any longer. Learn to do these things for yourself. Take the world in your own hands.' And we are. We're beginning to evolve into this great human spirit." She lay down again. "I think you'd better go now. My pulse is speeding up."

I lingered a moment at the door, then blew her a kiss good-bye.

PART II

A POLITICS FOR CRAZY OPTIMISTS

IN SPITE of everything, there's a smell of hope in the air. Admit it and you'll be called a crazy optimist.

It could be worse. All during the 1950s and most of the 1960s (according to at least one of the great newsmagazines), people were either "tough-minded" or "fuzzy-minded." Any optimism about human possibilities or hope for the gentler persuasions secured you the "fuzzy-minded" label. To be "tough-minded" you needed only pessimism, distrust of all human motives and belief in force or threat of it to achieve "realistic" ends. Well . . . events since early 1968 have conspired to take some of the smug certainty out of "tough-mindedness."

Still, I hesitate to come out against pessimism. History, a formidable opponent in any debate, so often manages to choose the negative side where human wisdom is concerned. Therefore, I'll only suggest, with all the diffidence I can command, that there are fuzzy-minded pessimists as well as fuzzy-minded optimists, and that today the former may be the more dangerous of the two. In times that demand swift change, pessimism can easily become a socially acceptable way of hoisting the white flag. And what a surrender—when the stakes are nothing less than mankind's survival on earth.

Politics may be the art of the possible, but it is no art at all without visions of what has hitherto been deemed impossible. The next three stories are about power and persuasion. The first shows Robert Kennedy in a bizarre trap of compromise and deception. This is followed by a modest manifesto for a different kind of power and then by an experiment in the politics of the human heart.

ROBERT KENNEDY, ROSS BARNETT

FOR FOUR DAYS in late September of 1962, this nation balanced on the edge of a state-sized civil war. Many thousands of people were involved: national leaders, soldiers, sheriffs, United States marshals, students, college professors and administrators, state legislators, extremists, ordinary citizens. In the end, two were killed and hundreds injured. This light toll was no less than a miracle in view of the situation's explosive potential.

The riot at the University of Mississippi was, in fact, the most serious domestic crisis during Robert Kennedy's term as Attorney General of the United States. Along with Mississippi Governor Ross Barnett, Kennedy played the major role in this near-catastrophe. The way he played it gives us a sharp picture of his fiber and his style. Undoubtedly Kennedy was instrumental in preventing a massacre at Ole Miss and a series of battles that could have spread even beyond Mississippi's borders. But there was hesitation and expediency along with his idealism and resolve.

Perhaps this was inevitable. *As it turned out, not a single person involved was aware of all that was going on; nobody could realize the possible consequences of his own actions.*

Two other *Look* editors flew with me to Mississippi the

day following the riot. After several days at Ole Miss in Oxford, we split up. T George Harris went to Jackson, the state capital, where he would pursue the stories of the Governor and his staff, newspapermen, members of the Citizens' Council and representatives of the state's more moderate leadership. Christopher S. Wren remained in Oxford, where he interviewed National Guardsmen, U.S. officers and men, college teachers and administrators, students, ministers and townspeople. I proceeded to Washington, where I concentrated my efforts on the Justice Department team, including U.S. marshals, officials and, most especially, Attorney General Kennedy himself.

The three of us remained on the assignment, comparing our findings, long after the other newspapermen had turned their cameras and their notebooks to other matters. The story that emerged was surprisingly different from what had appeared in the fast-breaking press.

Here is the situation that faced Robert Kennedy on Thursday, September 27, 1962, three days before the riot: Governor Ross Barnett had just about exhausted his legal means for preventing the registration of Negro James Meredith at the state university at Oxford. Kennedy, with his brother the President, was determined that Meredith, as he desired, be registered for the fall term. Unknown to Robert Kennedy, a group of Mississippi segregationist leaders were secretly planning to form a wall of unarmed bodies that would not yield until knocked down and trod upon by federal officers. Many segregationists were prepared to go to jail. Many were ready to fight with fists, rocks and clubs. Some resolved to stand until shot down. Others planned to defy the orders of their leaders and conceal pistols on their persons. Later, no one who understood this "wall of flesh" strategy estimated that less than "hundreds" would have been killed had the plan been carried out. One segregationist leader put the figure as high as 20,000.

But there was another twist to the story. We found out that, while Governor Barnett was encouraging the efforts of the segregationists to keep James Meredith out of the university, he was secretly suggesting schemes to Robert Kennedy that would let Meredith in.

By noon that Thursday, a great force had gathered at Ole Miss to repel the federal "invaders." Barnett and Lieutenant Governor Paul Johnson were there. Near the university's east gate, some 250 state troopers and county sheriffs were lined up, surrounded and infiltrated by a restless crowd of more than 2,000 students and others. All were waiting for James Meredith and whatever U.S. marshals he might have with him.

During this dangerous impasse, Robert Kennedy awaited a call from Ross Barnett, who, through a representative earlier that day, had suggested a way out. The call did not come. At 2:50 P.M., Washington time, Kennedy took the initiative and put a call through to Barnett.

"Hello," said Kennedy.

"Hello, General. How are you?" Barnett asked hospitably.

Previously the Governor had been intractable. Now he was worried about the contempt-of-court hearing coming up the next day. He knew that, if he did not let Meredith into Ole Miss, he might face a huge fine and possibly jail. He was also beginning to get sober council from the state's moderate leadership, who backed his principles but wanted to avoid a bloodbath. Barnett got right down to the business of his plan, which would allow him to be overwhelmed by the federal marshals while crying, "Never," for the segregationists' benefit.

The plan called for Barnett and Johnson to stand at the university's gate, backed up by unarmed state patrolmen. Kennedy would have Chief U.S. Marshal James McShane and 25 to 30 marshals bring Meredith to the gate. Barnett would refuse to let Meredith in. At this point, McShane would draw his gun, and the other marshals would slap their hands on their holsters. Barnett would then step aside and allow Meredith to register. The Mississippi highway patrol would maintain law and order. In his talk with Kennedy, the Governor worried about how the scene would look to "a big crowd." If only one man drew his gun, Barnett felt that he could not back down. So Kennedy reluctantly agreed to have all the marshals draw their guns. Under federal guns, Ross Barnett could surrender to prevent bloodshed.

Kennedy later explained to me that he knew his own "duty"—to uphold the courts and to do everything in his power to avoid bloodshed. He did not wish to use federal troops against, as he put it, "my fellow Americans." And, for the sake of a long-term solution, he wanted to leave law enforcement in state and local hands. The proposed scheme, however bizarre, would accomplish these purposes. Kennedy set about making plans to send Meredith and 25 marshals down to Oxford from their base at Millington Naval Air Station near Memphis.

But an hour later, Barnett called and asked for a postponement until Saturday the 29th. He seemed shaky and unsure of his control over his people. He put Lieutenant Governor Johnson on the phone. Johnson spoke briefly of "intense citizens," sheriffs and deputies not directly under state control. It might take time to "move them." Everything was held in suspense until Barnett phoned again. Be there at 5:00 P.M., Mississippi time, he told Kennedy. It was then 2:20 P.M. at Oxford. Barnett repeatedly promised there would be no violence.

A convoy of 13 green government sedans glided south from Memphis. Meredith, cool as always, rode in the back seat of one. At 3:35 P.M. Oxford time, Kennedy phoned Barnett to check on the situation. Now there was a change in Barnett's assurances. He spoke vaguely of keeping law and order "all over the state. . . . We always do that." Kennedy, greatly concerned, asked for more specific guarantees.

At that point, Kennedy could not possibly realize the Governor's dilemma. Barnett had set uncontrollable forces in motion. The brigade at the gate didn't know the Governor was negotiating surrender with "the enemy." Their job was to stop the federal marshals even at the cost of their lives. Barnett feared the hotheads would call the turn. At 4:35 P.M. Oxford time, he phoned Kennedy again. He said he was worried. He was nervous. He felt unable to control the crowd. The way things were going, he said, a hundred people might be killed, and that would "ruin all of us." It would, he said, be very embarrassing to him.

"I don't know if it would be *embarrassing*," Kennedy said. "That would not be the feeling." He hurriedly ended the conversation and radioed the convoy to turn back. It was then 30 miles from Oxford.

The next day, Friday, September 28, a circuit court gave Barnett until 11 A.M. Tuesday to purge himself of contempt. This meant, among other things, allowing Meredith to register. Now the Governor had his deadline. But

Robert Kennedy had a worse one. Getting Meredith into Ole Miss would be difficult and dangerous. But arresting the Governor of Mississippi in his state capitol!

Kennedy imagined the mob around the capitol building —troopers, sheriffs, "hotheads," and racists from all over. Two days before, ex-General Edwin Walker had spoken on the radio, calling for 10,000 volunteers from every state to come to the aid of Ross Barnett. Kennedy knew he would have to do everything in his power to get Meredith into Ole Miss by Tuesday morning. That Friday afternoon, he began meeting with military leaders to set up the forces that would be needed if Mississippi's defiance continued.

Just before noon the next day, a clear, early-autumn Saturday in Washington, Kennedy got a call from Jackson. He was not expecting any change, and none was forthcoming. Kennedy put down the phone and looked around grimly. "We'd better get moving," he said, "and get in there with the military."

At 12:15 P.M., he reached the President at the White House. The President told him to come over. Before leaving, the Attorney General shook his head and said softly to Edwin Guthman, his press secretary, "Maybe we waited too long."

At the White House, the President, with his brother and other advisers, set to work on military planning and on a TV address to the nation, tentatively set for Sunday night. Meanwhile, Governor Barnett was on the phone again with a new charade. He proposed that on Monday morning, he, Johnson, the troopers and sheriffs stand defiantly at the entrance to Ole Miss. While they waited, Meredith would be sneaked into Jackson, where facilities would be set up to register him. A "surprised" Barnett would complain bitterly of federal trickery. But on Tuesday, he would allow Meredith to come to Ole Miss. He promised the President that the highway patrol would maintain law and order.

All Saturday afternoon, the men in Washington considered the proposal. In a 7:00 P.M. telephone call, the President himself and Governor Barnett agreed to the plan. Robert Kennedy returned to the Justice Department, then went home around 10:00 P.M. Just after he left his office, the phone rang. It was Barnett. "Well, here we go again," Ed Guthman thought, as Barnett was told he could reach the Attorney General at home.

Guthman was right. The Governor called off the plan. It would be too politically embarrassing. Robert Kennedy's anger rose. This seemed a clear breach of an agreement between the Governor and the President. But the conversation ended amiably, with the understanding that the federal marshals would arrive with Meredith at Oxford Monday morning—in force. Barnett said he would phone again Sunday at 11:00 A.M. Washington time.

That Saturday night, many men were on the move. Troop transports flew through the darkness from North Carolina to Memphis. Racial agitators drove toward Oxford from as far away as Los Angeles. During a night football game in Jackson between Ole Miss and Kentucky, Ross Barnett was told that the President had federalized the Mississippi National Guard. Events were closing in on Barnett from both directions.

Sunday, September 30, was another beautiful day in Mississippi and in Washington. Robert Kennedy and his Mississippi task force were at work by 9:00 A.M. Tuesday's deadline pressed them hard. Now Kennedy was considering putting Meredith on the campus that Sunday. He knew that most of those coming to fight the government did not expect the action until Monday or Tuesday.

Then Ross Barnett was on the phone with yet another scheme. It was, basically, Thursday's charade, but on a grandiose scale. On Monday morning, October 1, he would wait at the university gate, backed by a phalanx of state troopers, who would be backed by sheriffs, who would be backed by citizens—all without guns. Meredith should arrive with a large army force. The Governor would read a proclamation barring him from Ole Miss. Then Kennedy's men should draw their guns. Barnett would surrender, and the troopers would clear a way for Meredith to enter.

Kennedy spoke to Barnett in a cold, controlled tone. He said the Governor had broken his agreement with the President. Barnett was responsible, Kennedy said, for more than his own political future. The Attorney General then shifted to a new tack. Unless the Governor cooperated, he said, and helped maintain law and order while Meredith went on campus, the President would go on television and inform the country that Barnett had broken his word. To prove it, the President would reveal all the behind-the-scenes dickering.

This threat had a devastating effect. The Governor's resistance melted away. Again and again, Barnett asked that the President say nothing on TV that would unveil the nature of the secret phone calls.

Kennedy suggested that Meredith be flown onto the campus by helicopter on Monday, while U.S. marshals and state troopers, working together, controlled the crowd. Barnett, who knew of the secret wall-of-flesh plans for that day, voiced a fear that on Monday, hundreds of people would be killed. He spoke of Mississippi's mood and of the hundreds of agitators on their way from other states. Because of Monday's danger, the two agreed that Meredith should be brought in before dark that afternoon and that the state highway patrol help get him on campus and maintain law and order.

So ended the strange negotiations between Robert Kennedy and Ross Barnett. The violence was only beginning.

A NEW LIBERAL MANIFESTO

THE OLD-LINE LIBERAL has failed. He has become, in fact, conservative or even reactionary. No longer does he press for the kind of deep-down, thoroughgoing reform the times demand. He creates, instead, a vacuum of positive leadership that today's young people lament and extremists exploit. Worst of all, he stuns us with dullness, offering a dreary future that seems to hold only more material goods and more entertainment for more people.

What went wrong? Yesterday's liberal became today's conservative by clinging to once-successful policies long after the conditions that made them successful had changed. In 1933, for example, the labor unions needed help to survive and grow, the poor needed massive direct relief, the federal government had to take on a new role and intervene in the crucial affairs of the time. To back those positions then excited humane hopes and stirred humane actions. To uphold them now may serve the status quo.

That is a simple explanation for the recent liberal malaise. But we can go deeper. Many liberals suffered a disabling flaw. Their liberalism did not extend below their eyebrows. That is to say, they were liberals of doctrine, ideology and the intellect. Too often, they were reactionaries of the feelings.

The old liberal sent money down South to keep Martin Luther King marching through Georgia. That suited the liberal's doctrine. And the action was far away. But when a black family moves in next door, he discovers a new doctrine in his guts. The fund-raiser-for-liberal-causes sings an unexpected, new theme when asked to show a loving interracial couple on the TV series he produces. The above-the-eyebrows liberal argues that racial prejudice is economic, sociological, anything but really human. "Whether I want my daughter to marry one is entirely beside the point."

It was never beside the point. A "belief" that doesn't go as deep as the deepest human feeling is not worth having. An inner lie, unperceived by the liar, can spread confusion and suffering. Whatever his doctrine, a person out of touch with his own feelings is out of touch with the true effects of his actions on others. He falls prey to the arrogance of distance. He may try to rebuild the ghettos from the top down, just as he tried rebuilding Vietnam from 30,000 feet. He is the most dangerous animal in the world, this emotional amputee. Living by ideas alone (no matter how "noble" the ideas), he could watch children and women maimed for the sake of a slogan. He never dreams that neither slogans nor any other abstractions have anything to do with morality. He might find it hard to understand that moral actions exist only on the ground floor of personal feelings and being, where individuals can reach out and touch their friends and loved ones, their fellow citizens and the inhabitants of bamboo huts in Southeast Asia.

After 300 years, the American Negro finally reached the

point (helped to some extent by old-time liberals) where he could say it like it is. The young militants said it: "We hate and fear you, white man. We don't want your sterile, twisted life. We want to feel pride in our blackness. We want to wear our hair natural. We want to build communities for ourselves that reflect *our* way of living and being in the world." Here was a perfect opportunity for a national black-white confrontation on the level of feeling. "Yes," the white liberals might have said, "we hear you, black man, and we feel uneasy. We feel guilty, and we resent that. We also resent you (after all we've done for you) for making trouble. Why can't you just fit into our way of life—dress neatly, brush up on your diction, visit our museums? We know we're supposed to like you, and we do, from a distance. But when you get too close to us or our women, we get a funny feeling in our stomachs. Maybe it's fear, and just a little hate, too, like you feel for us. So where do we go from here?"

Starting on this or any other honest, feeling level, members of both races can get beyond race to respect and even love. This has happened in interracial confrontation sessions around the nation. Such experiments have shown that reconciliation is possible only after an open and generally quite painful airing of emotions. There seems to be no way to tiptoe around on the edges of hypocrisy, politeness and sweet reason.

The young black militants did their part. They set up their half of an honest racial encounter. But the white liberal leaders kept whatever real feelings they had under wraps. They responded, instead, with measured words of caution and restraint. Later, as if referring to something else, they spoke out heatedly against "crime and violence in the streets." This monstrous response left the Negroes hanging in midair, frustrated and prone to even more violent outcries. It created the bizarre situation in which many informed Negroes now respect the racist ex-governor of Alabama more than the President of the United States. At least they know where George Wallace stands and what he really feels.

Modern technology draws us all close to one another. The acts of one man can rapidly and drastically alter the lives of people everywhere. In today's small world, we need to know more about a political leader than his ideas and pronouncements. We must know the man all the way through. This calls for radical reform in political style and content:

• *The new liberal will engage in a new politics of open encounter.* Doing the things now deemed necessary to achieve high office makes a man unworthy of that office. The candidate schemes, manipulates, lies, veils his true sentiments, appeals to friendship and loyalty for ulterior ends. Upon taking office, the candidate assures himself, he will change. A man is shaped by his actions, however, and rarely is able to turn away from what has just brought him success.

Perhaps the nation is ready for a new type of candidate. John F. Kennedy comes quickly to mind. He did plenty of political manipulation and infighting. But he never lost a certain charming candor. During the 1960 campaign, he told *Look* Editor in Chief William Attwood (then on the Kennedy team) there was one thing he swore he would never do: he would never wave his arms or gesticulate in a phony political manner. "Jack Kennedy could never pretend to be somebody he wasn't," Attwood wrote.

Barry Goldwater, no liberal in the traditional sense, was another candidate who didn't mind revealing himself. Bluntly, and with a minimum of compromise, he told the Republican convention and the nation just what he felt about war, peace and extremism. What more generous gift can we expect? The American people had a chance to reject his honestly avowed policies (only to watch helplessly as the most crucial of them later were put into effect by a "liberal" who avowed the precise opposite). But Goldwater's honesty gained respect.

Asking every candidate to reveal his deepest being and live an exemplary life is no frivolous matter. Practical men who might dismiss the notion as naïve may not have accurately judged the mood of the new generation. Not just radicals or fringe types, but most college students today seem to be deeply disappointed by the whole game of politics as it has been played. They are eager for leaders who are open, honest and aware. This seems at least as important to them as the "issues."

Disillusionment with traditional politics and politicians does not stop with the young. The decisive victories of inexperienced movie stars over experienced political figures have bemused the experts. But some observers have long recognized that a vote *for* a celebrity may be a vote *against* traditional policies. Near the end of the 1966 Brown-Reagan campaign in California, the Brown forces sponsored TV commercials contrasting the two candidates' political experience. Brown was shown through the window of his office, obviously late at night, pondering affairs of state. This was followed by a shot of a Reagan movie poster, accompanied by a little homily on experience and the lack thereof. The commercial probably increased Reagan's landslide margin. Rightly or wrongly, the last thing Californians wanted was all that "political" experience.

The excitement generated around Senator Eugene McCarthy, whose campaign seemed "amateurish" to the hardened ones, is another sign that the old political pro may be nearing the end of his reign. And whatever happened to the old pro's predictions about the ability of an incumbent to squash dissent?

The party and convention machinery is something else. When the national conventions approach, people of truly liberal persuasion may feel a deep sense of shame, for these performances represent much of what is worst in our culture. True, they are epic events, especially now that they are staged for color TV. But they are epics of skulduggery. Watching them, young people learn that the podium is for bombast, not truth-saying; that real leverage is to be gained cynically, behind closed doors; and that, anyway, most of the pork-barrel power up for grabs is irrelevant to the nation's future and unhealthy for whoever wins it.

Someday in the future, new liberals may help create a party that is a *party*—open, honest and even joyful. Party meetings will be of value *in themselves,* not just for whatever external power can be gained from them. The way people act at the meetings will serve as a model for how they will act in office.

This is not so utopian as it sounds. It may even be possible for some present-day candidate to subvert one of the parties toward openness and encounter. He could start simply by being himself. Even now, anyone who cuts through the sham and scheming, who is entirely honest about his actions, motives and feelings, might well electrify the voters and become a real threat to the pros.

• *The new liberal will tackle issues that are now largely ignored.* Back in February 1965, Peter F. Drucker proposed in *Harper's* that the real political issues of the coming age would be not the traditional economic and power-bloc struggles but the metropolis and the schools. His proposal startled at the time, but already seems commonplace. Yet many liberals still spin their wheels over issues that were largely resolved years ago, while not even acknowledging matters of great importance to the new generation.

The Issue Gap reveals itself in the words of opinion pollsters, who turn us from the future by scanning only that part of the horizon where they got blips in the past. Their stodgy questions elicit stodgy answers and encourage the view that Americans are stodgy people. Not too long ago, a well-known polling institute devised a long list of proposals that people would rate as to their importance. The original draft of the poll contained hardly anything that could not have been answered in the 1930s. A *Look* editor was asked to contribute additional items and did so, with a bias toward the under-twenty-fives. Among the suggested new items: encourage private enterprise to take responsibility for social programs; devise new regulations to prevent modern automation and communications techniques from abrogating individual rights; legalize marijuana; liberalize abortion laws; remove archaic sex-restriction laws; increase responsible research with psychedelic drugs; protect individual freedom in dress and hairstyle;

rush development of the electric car; rush research into more effective educational methods.

The poll was never taken. And face it, the old-line liberal would consider many of the above items outside the purview of responsible liberalism—which is one reason why liberalism as now generally practiced has become irrelevant. But these matters *are* being discussed and debated by the brightest of the young and by concerned people of all ages. Whether the new liberal agrees or disagrees with the items is not the main point. That he become relevant is.

• *The new liberal will not do things to or for other people, but will create conditions in which people can do things for themselves.* If people could just be given plenty of food and housing, the old liberal insisted, culture and the arts would flourish. Cynics have poked fun at this notion ever since poor English miners, moved into model housing, used their bathtubs to store coal. The evidence grows, however, that changing the total environment does change human behavior or even human "nature." But just giving things to people or "exposing" them to culture isn't enough. In fact, one-way good-doing often accomplishes the opposite of what is desired. Welfare, for example, somehow evolved into a system that would methodically reward people for acting poor and thus shape them into a lifelong pattern of poverty.

What is most important in environmental change is that the individuals involved must have key roles in their own destiny. For instance, life in the ghettos would be dramatically improved if residents could buy public housing. The government would have to take the risk of insuring bank loans at standards previously considered unacceptable. Banks would have to act enthusiastically, not just for public service but for private profit. Such a program would be ambitious and exciting. The possible rewards are huge. Against them, the risks dwindle.

Some businessmen already are acting to help people grasp their own destiny. In Detroit, the Ford Motor Company is recruiting among the hard-core unemployed. Ford has thrown out the dreaded written tests, the education and background requirements that have stood like barbed wire between "disadvantaged" people and good jobs. Research by the National Association of Manufacturers and others shows that it may soon be as cheap to train all people who come through the door as it is to set up elaborate screening procedures to keep some people out.

The welfare mess, bad as it is, can be straightened out by spirited liberal action. A reformed program would divorce itself from narrow middle-class notions of what is nice and proper. It would stop punishing recipients for acting "sharp" or "prosperous" (buying a tape recorder or a guitar on welfare money). It would give bonuses for voluntary educational efforts. More important, it would push and even sponsor basic change in education. The stultifying activity (sitting through lectures, for example) that now passes for schooling is hardly worth the time welfare recipients, or any others, spend on it. A new kind of education, combining imaginative technological aids with a more relaxed, open relationship between educator and learner, already is becoming available. Learners will stand in line for it.

What about foreign affairs? The Vietnam war, a mistake in almost anybody's terms, has provided a classic example of what can go wrong and what can go right. This war made us forget who we are. The new liberal will remember that America's genius lies in its pervasive peacetime influence. Guns, planes and bombs are not what can give us our real ultimate victory. The lesson of the years since World War II is that, when nations start reaching our level of technology and prosperity, they can be our friends—no matter what ideology they proclaim. The new liberal will work to create world prosperity, not to boss distant nations or to serve as an ideological cop. He will encourage free communications and open encounter overseas just as he does within these borders. He will strengthen the American example and continue the American experiment. He will seek peace.

• *The new liberal will see racial integration as a two-way process.* The old liberal always assumed that integration meant the Negro moving into white middle-class society, taking on white middle-class values and enjoying the material and aesthetic fruits of white middle-class culture. It's hard to imagine anything more arrogant, unfeeling and blind. If the present and future have anything to tell us, it's that the rigid, fragmented, uptight white middle-class life just won't work in this complex, richly interwoven, constantly shifting new technological age. The black culture has flaws; it is defensive and shot through with bitterness. But it has qualities this country now desperately needs. In the ghettos, you can find a rare sense of community and brotherhood, a rich awareness of what's up on the block—just what is lacking in white suburbia. Pallid and sterile, the suburbs could use a large portion of what the Negro calls "soul." This ubiquitous term sums up the

Negro's adaptation to a unique experience. It combines an easy access to authentic emotions with an ability to laugh or sing at adversity. Soul is really neither bitter nor sweet, but *salty*. This saltiness and emotionality has strong appeal for many of the younger generation.

The new liberal may well content himself with helping set up conditions in which the Negro can create his own culture—in the ghettos or elsewhere. (If anyone insists on doing missionary work—a dubious effort—he might turn to the white suburbs; there he will find the "race problem" at its worst.)

The flowering of Negro culture—in literature, the arts and the politics of feeling—can enrich all of American life and further an impulse toward integration in reverse. The impulse is already here, as is known by every liberal who listens to the music of the Beatles and Aretha Franklin as well as the press conferences of official Washington.

• *The new liberal will use all available avenues, new as well as old, for reform.* This may mean *relatively* less reliance on the federal government. The liberal reforms now needed are too vast, too complex and too subtle for government alone. Today's liberal will welcome the full participation of corporations, foundations, unions and professional groups in the great works of the time. He will repudiate forever the "public sector" vs. "private sector" polarization of John Kenneth Galbraith. Behind Galbraith's formulation lies the assumption that public agencies (outside the self) are and will always be virtuous while private impulse (the inner self) is selfish and evil. To recognize this split in most societies is one thing. To accept it as inevitable is another. The new liberal works toward new social structures in which there may be less and less contradiction between private impulse and the public good. In a sense, that's what the new liberalism is all about.

• *Allied with science and technology, the new liberal will welcome the responsibilities of creation.* Most scientists agree that eventually we shall be able to accomplish *anything* we can think up. Such things as traveling to the planets, controlling weather, conquering disease and transplanting the bodily organs are clear on the horizon. Much more lies just beyond: control of heredity, computers with "intelligence" and "feelings," and more. Already, men are making God-like decisions. (Heart transplants provide a dramatic example.) There is no way to escape the challenge. *Not* making decisions is also a choice. The new liberal will embrace rather than fear technology. He will put the liberal's traditional humanitarianism to perhaps its sternest test: making science man's servant, not his master.

• *The new liberal won't just protest, but will build anew.* Sometimes, it seems there's no way to make your voice heard except on the streets. Militant protest often serves the democratic process well. But it generates negative side effects. Opposition may be strengthened; positions, polarized. Worst, the protester may come to define (and limit) himself by what he opposes. As for change by overthrow—it generally ends with a new boss replacing the old.

To change things best, new liberals will build their own models of the future next door to the Establishment or even inside it. They will invite communication and interaction with the older order. They will assume such interaction is possible.

Taking this affirmative position, many experimental groups already are influencing attitudes and events. Student-led colleges are quietly reshaping their parent organizations. Experimental institutes are creating new modes of thought and action. In Washington, D.C., the Institute for Policy Studies is becoming, in the words of Resident Fellow Arthur I. Waskow, "not just an ordinary research center because it's committed to the idea that to develop social theory one must be involved in social action and in social experiment. And therefore, the Institute stands on the bare edge of custom. . . . It creates tension within the American legal and social system." Creating this sort of tension has always been the mark of true liberalism.

Some would-be young liberals say it is mischievous to spend energy working on new and more joyful ways of living while an unjust war is going on. But they miss a crucial point: peace is not simply the absence of war. It is an affirmative condition that must be built and rebuilt brick by brick. It must hold the excitement, the challenges to the human spirit, the opportunities for commitment traditionally associated with war. When men who might become adventurers or generals can find peacetime pursuits worthy of their energy and potential, they no longer will be sucked up in the madness of mass killing. Building peace is every bit as important as protesting war.

It is quite possible now to make a fresh start, to turn all the old limitations inside out. Unparalleled power is coming into our hands from science and technology. If only we act together, we can do with it what we will. Modern communications and transportation have multiplied and quickened human interaction. A model of something new and successful may be seen almost instantaneously throughout the world. The old social forms are crumbling, but this only opens the way for creating better new ones. The problems of physical survival in the advanced nations have just about been solved, forcing us all up against that formidable question: What—other than working and reproducing—is human life *for?* The new liberal will beware of timid expectations. The possibilities, if startling, are clear: in peace, we have at hand the resources, the energy and the talent to make each American city a festival, to make the entire country a garden, to find new ways for each individual to develop his capacities to the fullest.

The times cry out for audacious, joyful experiment. Even that crusty, tough-minded old futurist, Herman Kahn, recently remarked: "It takes very few people to change history. The question is, will the change be for good or bad?" The new liberal will take up the challenge. Not by his doctrine, but by his life and works, he will help change history for the good.

HOW TO HAVE A BLOODLESS RIOT

BEFORE THE CONFRONTATION begins, I am filled with dread. I stand around with the others, holding a cup of coffee. The talk is polite, subdued. But my hands are cold, my mouth is dry, and there's a strange tingling in my nostrils; I can hardly taste the coffee. I know what's ahead: anxiety, intractability, fury. I know what it's like to share a black man's nightmare, realizing that for him there's no waking up from it. Hours of pain. A white man crying for the first time since childhood. (The tear ducts are clogged, and all the channels for expressing grief have long been blocked by something as rock-hard and corrosive as desert salt. How it hurts when the stream of sadness forces its way through and the jagged, aching sobs break out—*at last.*) I also know about the eventual joy and the boisterous, crazy humor that sometimes helps us over the worst obstacles. But that's later. Right now, I'm not at all sure I'm ready for the dive into truth and reality. I turn to Price. He has been watching me. A certain smile tells me he has guessed my thoughts. He walks over and says, "How're you doing?"

He is Dr. Price M. Cobbs, a black psychiatrist and co-author (with his colleague, Dr. William H. Grier) of *Black Rage*. Dr. Cobbs and I co-led our first racial confrontation group in July 1967, the summer of the worst ghetto riots. Since then, we and teams we've trained have held confrontations under the auspices of various institutes, church groups, school systems and police departments. The group here is meeting at the headquarters of the Humanist Institute in San Francisco. All this activity is part of a growing national movement of racial confrontation. Our own formula is simple. We hope that each group will have black and white co-leaders. We insist that no racial confrontation be led by a white alone. We try for extended sessions; the most powerful format, we have found, is the 24-hour marathon. We demand commitment beyond the confines of the group. If something is learned, if a heart is changed, we urge the change be reflected on the job, in the community, in politics. Our ground rules are equally simple. We ask that everyone be completely honest and that they deal openly and immediately with their feelings.

The confrontation begins. There are 16 of us. Among us are a black welfare mother, a white cop, a well-to-do white matron, a black Vietnam veteran, a Mexican-American woman, a Black Panther. Within an hour, the group explodes as the Black Panther takes the floor. He calls the policeman a pig, chides a black woman for not wearing her hair natural and demands all-black groups. Blacks, he says, should never reveal themselves in front of whites. He rises to his rhetoric; he is wearing an "I'm black and I'm proud" button. The other blacks pick up phony vibrations. "Hell, man, you're so deep in the rhetoric you don't know *what* your feelings are." Price Cobbs zeros in: "When you walked in the door this morning, here's the feeling you gave me: it was like, 'Last night I was black. But, hell, this Price Cobbs has got this set here with some ofay chicks.

Let's go and get it on, man. Hell, I hope they don't catch me with the camera while I'm grooving.' " It is a moment of comic deflation. The Panther's mouth opens, but no words come out. The blacks laugh; they howl. The Panther becomes very serious. He goes to each black in the room and asks if they agree, if they think he is "gaming on them." One after another, they answer yes. The Panther listens carefully. "I haven't heard this before," he says. "I'm impressed. . . . I can't afford not to have you."

The blacks dominate the early hours of the confrontation, demanding honesty from each other, "getting the brothers together." "The blacker I am, man, the more brothers I love," Price Cobbs says. "Uncle Toms, Baptist preachers, militant Panthers, cats who have copped out, people on welfare." Beneath all the abrasiveness is a deep caring and sense of fraternity that is not lost on the whites. "Why—you people," the white matron says haltingly, "have a warmth I've never felt in my whole life."

To get the whites together, just to get them out of the armor built by lifetimes of rationalization, is not so easy. We spend hours working with a young white liberal. He starts out very Christian, full of love for all humanity. He wants to lead black-white groups himself. The blacks don't trust his bland assurances; they sense he has no access to his real feelings. We all stay with him, digging for a level of reality beneath that iron-plated, liberal-Christian armor. At last, we are all there with him as he shouts his hatred at every black in the room, at some of the whites. The group is in full voice. The sound rises in Wagnerian crescendo. It is frightening, wildly hilarious and somehow liberating. The sound deafens, but it is a better sound than sirens and riot guns. It is the sound of truth, a rare thing these days.

In our groups, we haven't found a white who isn't prejudiced or a black who isn't angry. So when our liberal Christian reveals, after the shouting dies down, that he physically fears the black Vietnam returnee, then tells him, "And, yes, I could—I *will* kill you if you don't get off my back," we are not surprised. We are glad it has been brought out into the open. Some people are horrified that such words are actually spoken, that a supposedly civilized Negro can yell, "Honky, racist, dog, pig!" at a nice white professor. But that is the grammar of reality in this country. When left unspoken, it is no less real and far more dangerous. In the customary American dialogue, the only way a black man can adequately reveal the outrage and powerlessness he feels is by throwing a Molotov cocktail. The only way a white can insulate his life is by moving to some sterile suburb of the senses, out of reach not only of life's pain but of its fullness and joy.

We believe the leaders of the nation, the white men who make the decisions, are flying completely blind on race. They could read a hundred books on the subject and remain abysmally ignorant. To begin their education, they might spend hours of true encounter with a black mother, and weep with her as she tells of the day her four-year-old came home crying, "But, Momma, I don't want to be a nigger. Why do I have to be?"

In our groups, we never try for "integration." If there's any message, it's "Let the blacks get blacker, the whites whiter, the browns browner. Let every man be himself in full." When this happens, when we've all gone through the storms of denunciation and revelation and emerged on the other side, there is almost always a spontaneous outpouring of love. At last, beyond all "reason," the blacks weep for the whites. And the laughter is gentle, if loud, when our Panther pins his "I'm black and I'm proud" button on a white doctor who has displayed an inordinate amount of soul, and proclaims him an "honorary nigger."

Race is a powerful searchlight. It penetrates to the dark core of a nation's sickness. It illuminates individual neuroses. It makes obscure dialectics as sharp and clear as black and white. Price Cobbs and I have an outrageous dream, but one that is beautiful. It goes something like this: The solution to race contains within it the solution to almost everything else that is wrong with our society. If we here in America can lick our race problems, *then what can't we do?* The dream may be outrageous, but in these dangerous times, we have no alternative but to make it come true.

PART III

GROWN-UPS VS. PEOPLE

A GROWN-UP is the man standing next to you in the elevator with the briefcase and the hat. He is not wearing his suit; it is wearing him. You feel that he is —well—*purposeful.* It is not that he's *serious;* children at play are serious. It's just that the grown-up seems to do everything, even smile and joke, for reasons that can't be found within his own skin. He goes to work because, reads because, has children because, partakes of art and culture because, makes friends because, even makes love because. The perfect grown-up will someday be replaced by a computer. Meanwhile, he exists as a homunculus inside a role. That's why he rarely really listens to you; he's just waiting for you to cue the next line in that interminable script he mistakes for a life.

In all of this, the grown-up responds with remarkable submissiveness to forces he cannot name and would not recognize. The more he inadvertently renounces his inner self, the more he grows in self-importance. His humanity shrinks. He begins to care less for other people than for material objects, abstractions, symbols, lines on a map. Thus, he becomes more dangerous than the plague. For unarguable "reasons," in the service of noble "ends," he is willing, at last, to sacrifice his grandmother for a poem, his children for an impressive obituary and a generation of young men for few miles of scarred earth.

The main function of schools is to make grown-ups out of people.

We may be thankful, then, that most schools are blessed with humane inefficiency. Rare is the perfect grown-up. *People*—that is, individuals who are in touch with their own feelings and therefore the feelings of others—are on the increase within the institutions of education. They envisage a schooling that would not depend upon inefficiency for its fine moments. Here and there, perhaps only a little bit at a time, they are changing the schools, and the world.

TESTING VS. YOUR CHILD

"THERE'S A STORY in Greek mythology about the goddess Circe and how she turned strong, brave men into swine. I saw that happen in a classroom. I watched students—human beings—turned into swine."

The graduate student's eyes brimmed with anger. He was telling me about an experimental class at a large university, one of the few in which American students are encouraged to learn for the sheer joy of learning—without testing, without grading.

"The professor was uneasy about the whole thing," the graduate student, who taught in the experimental class, went on. "He wasn't sure that every member of his class had been reading exactly what he assigned them. So one morning, he walked to the front of the class, looked around and said, 'Get out a blank piece of paper and number it one through ten.' As the students realized what was happening, their faces changed. The light in their eyes dwindled to something shameful. The professor reeled off ten questions—factual, petty, simpleminded—and then asked that the papers be passed to the front. He said, 'As you all know, there are no tests or grades in this class,' and he tore the papers up. But the damage was done. He had reminded them just what he thought of them. He was the teacher. They were pupils—limited, slightly less than human, expected only to regurgitate facts and opinions that he had stuffed into them, subject to classification by a number or a letter. *Swine.*"

This professor was not alone in his need for reassurance, his desire for a simple, immediate way of measuring academic performance. Throughout the United States, to an extent undreamed-of in the long history of education, students are being tested, measured, analyzed, classified and segregated by their ability or inability to sit, pencil in hand, and check off "right" answers. As the process called "education" keeps getting lengthier and more crucial to the life of your child, the science of testing is outrunning the art of teaching. Your child's teacher stands in danger of becoming not a connoisseur of learning, but a custodian of examination.

This year alone, more than 100 million ability tests will be administered in American schools—and that's the least of it. Simply to list the number and variety of tests that surround your child's life is a task beyond our best statisticians and their machines. The testing that tiptoes tunefully on to the scene in kindergarten reaches a mad climax during high school's senior year. In New York State, for example, the college-bound senior is offered—in addition to everything else—the New York Regents exams, the College Entrance Examination Board tests, the American College Testing Program examination and the Advanced Placement exams. Tests of one sort or another will largely determine the college your child goes to, his job, his income, the people he meets, the person he marries and the destiny of your grandchildren.

The question is: Are tests up to such a responsibility? I have talked to a number of leading U.S. educators who feel they are not. These men are uneasy. They squirm in their seats, shake their heads, look off into the distance for some as yet unseen solution to their quandary: with education getting more and more expensive, parents—and legislators—are demanding a quick payoff. They want their money's worth of educational "improvements" in terms they can readily comprehend. They want test scores that are higher than the next school's or the next town's or the next state's. They want this year's fifth grade to outscore last year's fifth grade. They rarely stop to ask just *what* is being scored. They want, most of all, a good college or a good job for their children, and they fully expect the schools to get it for them—little matter *how*.

Teachers are caught in the squeeze. They must teach more children than ever before—practically the entire population of a continent-wide nation. They must teach them more than ever before. But *how?* In most cases—*though effective new learning methods are already available*—today's teachers are boxed into situations and methods that were outmoded 50 years ago.

What is the teacher to do? Generally he can come up with nothing better than assigning more and more homework, giving more and tougher tests and depending more helplessly than ever on scores of various kinds to sort out the sheep from the goats.

In such a situation, scores and grades take on a demoniac life of their own, having as little to do with true education as a graven idol has to do with true worship. Essentially freed from the process of learning, grades can serve a darker art, instilling fear and acceptance in those of our children whom the idolaters would call "low achievers" and showing "high achievers" the way to early cynicism. Listen to some of the bright ones—beautiful, weary fourteen-year-olds from an upper-income junior high south of San Francisco:

ELLEN: "If I brought home a bad report card, my mother would make me feel like a heel. She would say, 'After all I've done for you, all my effort and all my planning, and now you do this to me.' And I would feel guilty."

JOSH: "Dad would knock my teeth out."

FRANK: "My mother would probably cause the teacher to have a heart failure. She's done that before, you know. One time, she made it so tough on a teacher that he had a heart attack and had to resign for health reasons."

BILLY: "Don't blame teachers for piling on too much work, especially science teachers. It depends on who's ahead in the space race. If the Russians get a satellite up, they say, 'The Russians might get ahead of us,' and they give us an extra dose of homework. If we have a better satellite up, the science assignments ease off."

If our children seem cynical, it is because they see straight to the heart of adult motives. The uneasy adult critics of excessive testing rarely display such insight. They waste their voices crying, "Tyrant!" at the test makers, never stopping to think how much we depend on these good workmen to keep shoring up a house of learning that needs rebuilding from its very foundation. They play a losing game of quibbles with the test makers, seeking minute flaws in multiple-choice tests, gloating over the one question out of a thousand that seems to contain more than one "right" answer. This game merely pushes the test makers to falsify the world even further—presenting it as having no ambiguities or paradoxes whatever. Many writers and educators who start out attacking wanton testing end up waving the flag of surrender. In an article on the subject in *Mademoiselle,* Rita Hoffmann was forced to conclude that "objective tests of intellectual attainment and promise are the most useful instruments available for the maintenance of the present unwieldy system of higher education in the U.S. It is as foolish and fruitless to cry out against tests and IBM cards as it is to bay at the moon."

In her despair, Miss Hoffmann has bumped into the truth. Heavy testing is precisely what she calls it: an instrument of maintenance. It does make "the present unwieldy system" possible, delaying for a few more years, perhaps, the inevitable time of real educational reform. It is both symptom and cause of what is sickest in our schools.

The teacher who relies heavily on tests does not have to concern himself with the learning process. He can simply assign lessons, then later test his students to see what they have learned on their own. *This is not teaching.* He can continue to use the lecture method, that outmoded, one-way form of noncommunication that may be defined as the easiest way to get material from the teacher's notebook to the student's notebook without touching the student's mind. *This is not teaching.* He may go on giving great weight to midterm and final exams, which is not helping students diagnose their problems, but giving a test to give a mark. *This is not teaching.*

Educators who assume that only the threat of an exam can force students to learn lack faith in their own ability to teach. Here, with routine teaching methods, they may be right. They also lack faith in their students' ability to learn. Here they are wrong. Children are smart. Many prove it by continuing to learn and to enjoy learning in spite of all the pressures and inefficiencies of current educational methods. Many others prove it by devising ingenious ways to beat a game they do not respect. Actually, the present situation, with its heavy emphasis on tests and its insane pressure for grades, is less an invitation to learn than an invitation to cheat. Just as heavy testing is a symptom of what is wrong with our schools, cheating is a symptom of what is wrong with heavy testing.

Today, dishonesty in the service of the grade-point average is epidemic in the nation's schools and colleges. A Columbia University study of more than 5,000 students in 99 U.S. colleges found that at least 50 percent *admitted* cheating. William J. Bowers, the author of the study, estimated that an even greater percentage of students cheat in high school. A recent Junior Chamber of Commerce poll of over 100 public schools in Virginia showed that 70 percent of the schools had a "serious" cheating problem. A *New York Times* survey of a dozen city high schools indicated that cheating was on the increase, especially among students near the head of their class who are pushing for Ivy League berths. The results of these surveys should surprise no one who has comprehended the machinery of the assign-and-test system, in which grades have been divorced from true learning. Students may be morally wrong in cheating. Educationally, they are quite right. If they get away with it, they prove they have merit in coping with a poorly designed learning environment and, therefore, deserve to be admitted to a "tough" assign-and-test college where they can continue to do the same.

Our children are bright. They have developed a technology of cheating that brings into play fields as diverse as electronics and teen fashions. Radio transmitters that can send messages to miniature receivers disguised as hearing aids have been reported in North Carolina. A suburban New York high-school junior recently explained that the short-skirt fad had raised many girls' averages, since notes can be written on slips, which, she said, have not gone up so quickly as skirtlines. Teased hair is reputed to make a cozy nest for notes. "And have you noticed," a boy in the suburban class asked, "how many colds there are during tests? I saw one girl use seven marked-up tissues during one period."

Cheating, like war, brings out the worst and the best in our young people. One New York City junior-high boy told how he blackmailed a classmate upon finding him flipping through a book in the washroom during a test period. The blackmailer simply took the book as evidence and sold it back to the cheater for 50 dollars. A selfless spirit of mutual help, however, inspires many cheaters. They manage marvels of nonverbal communication—with coughs, grunts, body motions, ear tugging, foot tapping—so that classmates may share every possible little driblet of "right" information. One class reported success with the "Purloined Letter" gambit. They wrote the answers to a test on the corner of the blackboard before the period began. Even though proctors walked up and down the aisles throughout the test, they never noticed the obvious.

Teachers often respond to their students' ingenuity by playing at cops and robbers. Educational journals abound with advice on beating the cheaters at their own game. In *The Clearing House: A Journal for Modern Junior and Senior High Schools,* December 1964, Donald A. Wesley presents his colleagues with "Some Useful Tricks of the

Trade." He recommends that, during tests, the teacher position himself in the back of the room, in which case "tempted students are often deterred, as they cannot be certain whether or not they are being watched." The author faces up squarely to the crisis that arises when some students finish their tests early. "As pupils finish, it is best for the teacher to move about and collect papers rather than to permit a steady parade up to his desk. This restriction of pupil movement is desirable during an examination."

On a grander scale, Sherman N. Tinkelman of the New York State Education Department has outlined some of the security measures surrounding the Regents exams in language that brings back D-day, counterespionage, the invasion of Europe—*synchronize your watches, men:*

> Precautions are taken at every step to preserve the security and integrity of Regents examinations. The examinations are printed in the Department's own plant in Albany. They are packaged in sealed envelopes and are sent to the schools in locked steel boxes. The administration of the examination in each school, at a uniform time throughout the state, is under the direct supervision and responsibility of the principal, who is the official deputy of the State Education Department.

Mr. Tinkelman said that in a speech at a testing conference. His audience probably never questioned whether wartime security measures and locked steel boxes have any place in an educational endeavor. That a respected educator could speak of them without apologies to his listeners' sensibilities only underlines the madness of the prevailing educational climate.

And still the conflict escalates. Now educators are bringing what may be the doomsday anticheating weapon up onto the firing line. What is it? A computer programmed to detect collusion on multiple-choice tests. Recently, ten students at Howard University in Washington, D.C., were suspended after being confronted with the computer's icy accusation of cheating.

Yet it would be premature to bet against the students in the great cheating battle. As a matter of fact, they generally rise to each new and harsh anticheating measure with renewed vigor and ingenuity. The Columbia University study reveals that "courses in which students are watched closely during tests and exams are twice as likely to have had instances of academic dishonesty as those in which they are not. Furthermore . . . cheating is more likely to occur when rules and regulations governing the taking of tests and exams are stricter."

An experiment with a blind teacher in Detroit adds poignancy to the Columbia findings, showing again that the harder it is to cheat, the more students will cheat. Given equal opportunities to cheat on a blind instructor and a sighted one, students in the Detroit experiment cheated more than twice as much in the sighted instructor's class. The authors of the study concluded that "the American student's sense of fair play, as represented by his behavior relative to the blind, is very much alive."

Only the hypocritical or the poorly informed would prattle about some vague "moral degeneration" in today's students. Our children are simply responding—generally quite appropriately—to the world we have made for them. Finding themselves in a situation where grades are worshipped excessively for their own sakes, quite apart from the learning process, where pupils are treated as "the enemy" or as cold statistics, our children act as they are treated.

Their behavior has a clear and urgent message for those who would listen. The message points the way toward real change, toward a new kind of school in which cheating will virtually disappear. Perhaps the most striking findings in the Columbia study show what happens in contrasting learning situations. *Invariably, the better the situation, the closer the class to real reform in teaching, the less the cheating.* There is substantially less cheating in seminar or discussion classes than in lecture classes; substantially less cheating in courses with outside reading than in courses that depend on textbooks alone; substantially less cheating in small classes than in large classes; substantially less cheating in advanced than in elementary courses; substantially less cheating when grading is straightforward than when students are placed in competition with each other on a "curve"; substantially less cheating when fewer tests are given.

What are our young people trying to tell us? Improve the learning situation, their actions say, and you will reduce cheating at the same time you enhance learning. What would happen if we took their message to heart? Where would it lead our schools? Already a few adventurous educators are moving in a new direction, but they have to move cautiously, a few small steps at a time.

Strangely, when human life around the globe is turning topsy-turvy, when even such staid old institutions as banks and insurance companies are changing beyond recognition, most of our schools continue to cling to the past. The highly publicized New Curriculum movement, which has, among other things, forced bewildered parents to learn arithmetic all over again, is an admirable updating of subject content. But it is not real reform. To the contrary, whenever it makes elementary school more like college by splitting the world into rigid academic departments, it runs against reform. We have reached the historic point when it is time to put the world back together again, not to break it into even smaller pieces; to find connections, not divisions in the body of knowledge. Both school and college could well bear changing. Starting out from some imaginative experiments that have already proved successful, here are a few first steps toward the future:

1. *Teachers will assume every student can learn.* If the student is not learning, they will consider it their fault, not his. This truly revolutionary attitude springs largely from the programmed-instruction movement, founded by B. F. Skinner of Harvard in 1954. Since then, programmed instruction has had its ups and downs, but its new attitude toward the student has proved valuable time and again. By attending very closely to the learning process itself, by checking what has to be learned—at every step along the way—against the actual performance of the kind of students who will be learning it, programmers repeatedly come up with courses that assure almost every student at least 95 percent correct answers. Students work individually with simple teaching machines or programmed books. Some go faster than others. But all of them "get" what amounts to an "A."

When learning without error can happen, you have to throw all the books about testing out the window. The new situation comes to this: *anything you can test, you can program; anything you can program, you don't need to test.* The idea, of course, takes getting used to. Some teachers, still thinking of learning as something that has to be forced on children, cannot believe their senses when all children learn with ease and pleasure, when the fast ones burn through a semester's work in a few days. These teachers complicate the programmer's work by devising stratagems to slow their students' pace. "What they miss most of all is tests," programmer Dr. M. W. Sullivan told me. "Our earlier version of Programmed Reading contained no rests. This caused great anxiety among teachers. They felt they weren't in control of the situation. They found it hard to trust their children to learn just for the joy of it —*even though they were.* So we have put in so-called tests, and we have made them the happiest part of the program. The best story is going to be the 'test.' This makes the teachers happy and doesn't hurt the program at all."

Men like Sullivan challenge all American educators, whether or not they use the specific techniques of programmed instruction. By proving that children can learn more and faster than was ever thought possible, they demand that teachers critically examine and improve their own methods. This teachers can never do so long as they rely heavily on tests to bail them out of their predicaments.

2. *Teachers will use their precious time and talent actually teaching.* Teaching is two-way communication. Teaching is confrontation. It is not standing in front of a number of young people and droning out facts and techniques. Such bread-and-butter aspects of learning are best taught through programmed-instruction devices or by children coaching each other. Under the present setup, teachers often spend up to half their time (and I have seen this rise

to 90 percent) keeping the class in order. As learning becomes really exciting, the control problem disappears. Children can spend a great deal of their time working on individual projects rather than preparing for group tests. The teacher is then free to devote most of his time to individual or small-group instruction.

3. *Early education will be reemphasized.* Almost without exception, present-day educational reformers reveal their fascination with the high-school years, to the detriment of all-important early schooling. Their interest rises as the possibility of effective reform plummets. A conclusive body of research shows that the younger the child, the more effective and lasting will be any effort to teach him. True reform in schooling can begin only when increased money, attention and status are turned toward the school years that start at kindergarten or sooner.

4. *Testing—the baling wire that holds the present unwieldy system together—will be reduced to a bare minimum.* So long as the teacher can hide behind tests, he will not feel the urgent need for reform in teaching methods. So long as the student senses that tests and scores are what really count in school, he will not know the joy of real learning. So long as the school administrator knows his school is being rated by how well students perform on nationwide or statewide standardized tests, he will be inhibited from bold experimentation.

As it is, teachers and whole school systems are being shaped by last year's tests—what was asked on them and how it was asked. "If a standardized test is really important to children's future or to educators' prestige," Dr. Arthur F. Corey, long-time executive secretary of the California Teachers Association, told me, "I don't know of any way you can keep teachers from teaching for the tests. This is bound to block change."

Once educators gain faith in children's remarkable capacity to learn, once they bend their efforts to tapping this capacity, they will escape their dependence on these crude instruments. Final exams can easily be replaced by long-term projects or open-book exercises. Occasional quizzes may be given for the student's benefit in diagnosing his problems, not for the teacher's grade book.

If it is necessary to measure the nation's educational progress, the job may be done with polling or sampling techniques, so that no child or school will be singled out and shaped by the test results. A distinguished national committee, financed by the Carnegie Corporation, is now working out such an assessment program. Talks with the committee's chairman, Ralph W. Tyler, and U.S. Assistant Secretary for Education Francis Keppel have convinced me that his committee is trying to avoid the stultifying consequences that would follow if the program became a national test rather than a sample.

As for standardized college-entrance tests, evidence is heaping up that undue reliance on their scores closes certain college doors to students who would make campus leaders—or even "intellectuals." When college-admissions officers gain faith in human abilities, they will pay less attention to cold figures.

New faith in human abilities can lead to new ways of approaching human individuals. George Bernard Shaw pointed out that the main difference between a flower girl and a duchess is how she is treated. We have tried testing our children half to death. Perhaps it is time to treat them differently.

WHAT YOUR CHILD CAN TEACH HIS TEACHER

YOUR YOUNG CHILD can pick up a new language in a few months, understand advanced mathematical concepts, perceive infinitesimal variations in color and form. He loves nothing in life so much as learning. In spite of this, his teacher may have been led into a common error: he may believe he has more to teach the child than the child has to teach him. So believing, he may set out—with all the goodwill in the world—to fix limits on the child's perceptions, to train his torrential imagination along narrow, predetermined channels and, in short, to make a free-swinging learner into a well-behaved puppet.

Perhaps it is more than coincidence that the child's remarkable growth rate in intelligence starts to fall off just as he enters school. Dr. Benjamin S. Bloom, in his *Stability and Change in Human Characteristics,* shows that half of all intelligence increase generally comes before age four; the next 30 percent takes place between four and eight. That most people grow little in intelligence after eight would probably surprise no one who has had the chance to visit a number of elementary schools. Over the past years, I have spent a great deal of time in several hundred classrooms around the U.S. and have often talked with teachers about the mysterious change that occurs in children during their early school years.

Go into a kindergarten room. By and large, the five-year-olds are spontaneous, unique. Tell them to dance, and they move naturally with a sort of unorganized grace. Read them a story, and their eyes give you back its suspense, fear, laughter. We like to say their faces "light up" (a particularly telling phrase), and when we look into this illumination, we are not ashamed to let our own faces glow in return. All of this, we assume, is a natural condition of the very young.

Walk down the hall to a fourth-grade classroom. Very quickly, you will notice that something has been lost. Not so many eyes are alight. Not so many responses surprise you. Too many bodies and minds seem locked in painful self-awareness. This, too, we carelessly attribute to the natural order. It's just part of growing up.

But is it really? Is it really necessary for the human animal to lose in spontaneity and imagination as it gains in knowledge and technique? Must we shed the brightness of childhood as we put on the armor plating of age? The answer to these questions is by no means certain, but a growing number of educators and psychologists are betting that there is nothing *natural* about the relentless attrition of spontaneity and the slackening of the learning curve. New research suggests that the human brain can never be "filled up," but that it can be *trained* to be rigid, to reject the unfamiliar, to run on well-worn tracks. There is reason to suspect, in fact, that training to these ends often has been a major unacknowledged goal of formal education. Nothing malicious or capricious about this: until recently, our society has been stratified and specialized.

Look at it as a great stack of boxes. Individuals have had to be shaped and honed to fit into these boxes—fixed social roles, jobs and careers. People who would go right on learning—that is, changing—all lifelong might threaten the structure and stability of such a society. The schools served stability, helped fit individuals into boxes.

Now all this is changing. We are a people in flux. The old boxes no longer hold. Already workers are changing careers three and four times—and that is only the beginning. An onrushing technology, it appears, will require that most people go on learning most of their lives. Electronically controlled mechanisms will do the drudge's work; more and more of us will be called upon to be sensitive and creative. Under these circumstances, the schools may best serve society by serving the individual capacity to keep learning, to keep changing, to keep creating. Indeed, today's most innovative educators are seeking new ways toward those goals. For their guide, they are taking the child himself.

"Our children are our main data source," Dr. John I. Goodlad told me. One of the pioneers of the nongraded approach to schooling, Dr. Goodlad is director of UCLA's University Elementary School in Los Angeles. "By attending sensitively to what is unique as well as what is common in children, the teacher will not only *learn,* but also will provide education on a different model."

What happens when teachers start learning from children? At Dr. Goodlad's showcase school, I met one teacher who found she had to move far beyond all previous studies. Seeking a precise understanding of nursery-school behavior, June Patterson discovered that a child goes through several crucial steps in learning something as seemingly simple as galloping or caring for personal belongings. Adults can easily overlook these giant steps and assume a child is not learning anything. Miss Patterson and other teachers at the school are trying to catalogue as many of the specifics of learning as they can.

In a science class, I learned what exquisite observers young children can be when they are free to observe. "How would you describe this object?" science teacher Stanford Davis asked, holding up a wooden cylinder. "It's a long-round," a six-year-old girl said. "It like what came out of the inside of a tunnel," a boy added.

Davis held up what looked like a large black rock. "Who will come up and describe the properties of this object?" A girl with blonde pigtails came forward and took the object in her hands. "It's black, rough and heavy, yet in places, it's smooth . . . and it's white and it's red, too." "Is this *red?*" Davis asked. "I don't see—oh, yes. I would have called it black, but here the red is, all right."

Later I asked to see the rock. After quite a bit of searching, I made out the faintest tinge of red on one side. "When I first started using this object, I didn't see the red at all," Davis said. "But the kids spot it every time, quickly and easily."

Some new psychological studies reveal the young child's powers of perception. Dr. Rosslyn G. Suchman of the Institute of Human Development at the University of California at Berkeley showed me a card with five bright-yellow squares. "Which square is different?" she asked me. After a couple of minutes of staring, I pointed at one of them. "Notice how long it took you," she said. "In all the time I've used these cards, I've never found an adult as fast as the great majority of middle-class four- to seven-year-olds.

They're so fast that I'm still looking at the answer sheet when they've finished."

Dr. Suchman—who is the mother of two—showed me another set of cards, each having five geometric designs, one of which was barely different from the other four. "These aren't the hardest," she said. "While I was testing one four-year-old girl, I told her, 'These problems are getting harder.' She looked at me incredulously and said, 'Do you really think *these* are hard?' Later I said, '*Now* they're getting harder.' 'You think these are *hard?*' she asked me. 'Why, I could do them under the table.' She slid down under the table, and I broke up. I also redesigned the problems."

Children see the world pure and clear, without hypotheses. "It's a different and more exciting world than ours," Mrs. Suchman said. "Children come into the schools open and unique. If you took an interest inventory with the middle-class kid in kindergarten, my bet would be you'd find a wider range of interests than at any other time until he gets out of the educational system. He wants to know why waves break, why trains go, all about seashells and literature. Of course, he must become more sustained, more controlled in his interests. But if the price of control is deadening the interests of kids, it's too big a price."

Mrs. Suchman's husband, Dr. J. Richard Suchman, is the founder of Inquiry Development, an educational approach that helps children work out their own concepts of the way the world is. The teacher provides information and encouragement, but does not force his or any other theories on the children. "We believe children are tremendously motivated to do their own thinking," Dr. Suchman said. "Most artificial motivators we use on them—grades, prizes, adult approval—actually get in the way of the inner desire to learn. The whole idea of school achievement is tied in with this old system. Naturally the child wants 'achievement,' so he sets aside his own way of seeing, he betrays his own honesty, he stops pursuing meaning and starts reciting approved, adult answers.

"In our approach, there's no punishment for coming up with an idea that doesn't match the experts'. This way, we've learned just how inventive children can be. For example, fifth- and sixth-graders have worked out very good theories to explain sinking and floating. Without knowing anything about Archimedes' principle, just working from raw data, they've come up with explanations I consider in some ways more elegant and precise than Archimedes'. Even if they could just come up to his principle, I'd think it was pretty good, but they do even better. With this kind of thing going on, teachers *must* learn from their students, if only to keep pace with them."

The kind of freedom the Suchmans want for all children won't just happen. For one thing, after students have learned to play the old, adult-approved school game, they need time to get accustomed to freedom. They need teachers who are both patient and flexible, resilient and free-swinging. The usual critical line is that teachers are unwilling or unable to change creatively. My meetings with hundreds of them convince me this is not true. Today, as a matter of fact, many teachers seem eager for new ways to meet new challenges. It's just that the usual rigid classroom situation and the vague methods generally available to them make change difficult for even the best. That so many of them *are* searching seems remarkable. For example, English teachers and experts at a recent Dartmouth seminar recommended that teachers should say less and children, more in English classes. And the Western Behavioral Sciences Institute (WBSI) is discovering that students have unsuspected talents and knowledge when they are allowed to interact strongly with one another. In the WBSI educational games, students quickly become shrewd bargainers in international relations or politics. And, again, teachers learn from youthful strokes of insight. "Politics," one high-school junior mused, "seems to care about the wrong things." Even educators who might disagree on method and philosophy agree on the importance of the child as teacher—if they are educators who are actively interested in reform.

What can your child teach his teacher? Originality, open-mindedness, clarity of vision, adaptability, sensitivity, spontaneity, enthusiasm, joyfulness, grace. To this list might be added four items frequently mentioned to me:

1. *Fairness.* The young child's sense of justice may not be legalistic or sophisticated, but it is clear and strong. If two children are making a disturbance and only one is corrected, the whole class feels the wrong.

2. *Forbearance and loyalty.* The young child will go to heroic lengths to make allowances for teachers' failures. I watched one class in which the teacher seemed inexcusably cross and unjust. At playtime, a six-year-old girl told me: "Miss Jones isn't feeling good, that's all." Unfortunately, children learn from grown-ups more than the other way

around, so children eventually become as distrustful and intolerant as anyone else—i.e., they become adults.

3. *Wholeness.* Grown-ups are not really people. They are, as Saint-Exupéry has said so charmingly in *The Little Prince,* kings, generals, businessmen, geographers. Since they are biased and circumscribed by the roles they play, they act in limited, repetitive ways and are, in the words of the Little Prince, "certainly very odd." Children are children—that is to say, whole people. If we learn from them well, perhaps they will help us teachers, principals, stenographers, doctors, machinists, kings, generals and writers become people.

4. *How to learn.* Since the chief business of the future will be learning, and the main thing we'll have to learn is how to learn, it is about this business that the child can teach his teacher—and all of us—the most. We might well study this master learner in the environment that makes his remarkable performance possible. Watch the preschool child pick up something as simple as a handclapping game or as complex as spoken language. Observe the absence of grades, seating arrangements, verbal admonishments, lectures or even—whisper the word—teachers. Then note what is really needed for fast learning: an environment, whether it be people or things, that encourages the learner to respond freely, then somehow responds back to him. (When the baby first says, "Mama," *something happens.*) The world itself provides the responsive environment for the young child. Much can be done, and is being done, to make schools truly responsive in teaching the present stuff of education and more. In such schools, teachers and teach-

ing, as we now know them, may vanish, and teachers may have a chance to become, for the first time, real educators.

It is just possible, as a matter of fact, that the child is showing us the way toward an educational reform that will make all previous reforms seem trivial.

THE FUTURE OF EDUCATION*

THE TIME IS COMING, if it is not already here, when children can learn far more, far faster in the outside world than within schoolhouse walls. "Why should I go back to school and interrupt my education?" the high-school dropout asks. His question is impudent but to the point. The modern urban environment is packed with energy and information—diverse, insistent, compelling. Four-year-olds, as school innovators are fond of saying, may spend their playtimes discussing the speed, range and flight characteristics of jet aircraft, only to return to a classroom and "string some more of those beads." The sixteen-year-old who drops out of school may be risking his financial future, but he is not necessarily lacking in intelligence. One of the unexpected statistics of recent years comes from Dr. Louis Bright, Associate U.S. Commissioner of Education for Research. His studies show that, in large cities where figures are available, dropouts have higher average IQ scores than high-school graduates.

This danger signal is only one of many now flashing in school systems throughout the world. The signals say that something is out of phase, that most present-day schools

* With Marshall McLuhan.

may be lavishing vast and increasing amounts of time and energy preparing students for a world that no longer exists. Though this is a time of educational experiments, the real reforms that might be expected have as yet touched only a small proportion of our schools. Today's typical classroom—in physical layout, method and content of instruction—still resembles the classroom of 30 or more years ago.

Resistance to change is understandable and perhaps unavoidable in an endeavor as complex as education, dealing as it does with human lives. But the status quo may not endure much longer. The demands, the very nature of this age of new technology and pervasive electric circuitry, barely perceived because so close at hand, will shape education's future. By the time this year's babies have become graduates (if college "graduation" then exists), schooling as we now know it may be only a memory.

Mass education is a child of a mechanical age. It grew up along with the production line. It reached maturity just at that historical moment when Western civilization had attained its final extreme of fragmentation and specialization, and had mastered the linear technique of stamping out products in the mass.

It was this civilization's genius to manipulate matter, energy and human life by breaking every useful process down into its functional parts, then producing any required number of each. Just as shaped pieces of metal became components of a locomotive, human specialists become components of the great social machine.

In this setting, education's task was fairly simple: decide what the social machine needs, then turn out people who match those needs. The school's function was not so much to encourage people to keep exploring, learning and, therefore, changing throughout life as to slow and control those very processes of personal growth and change. Providing useful career or job skills was only a small part of this educational matching game. All students, perhaps more so in the humanities than the sciences and technologies, were furnished standard "bodies of knowledge," vocabularies, concepts and ways of viewing the world. Scholarly or trade journals generally held a close check on standard perceptions in each special field.

Specialization and standardization produced close resemblance and, therefore, hot competition between individuals. Normally the only way a person could differentiate himself from the fellow specialists next to him was by doing the same thing better and faster. Competition, as a matter of fact, became the chief motive force in mass education, as in society, with grades and tests of all sorts gathering about them a power and glory all out of proportion to their quite limited function as learning aids.

Then, too, just as the old mechanical production line pressed physical materials into preset and unvarying molds, so mass education tended to treat students as objects to be shaped, manipulated. "Instruction" generally meant pressing information onto passive students. Lectures, the most common mode of instruction in mass education, called for very little student involvement. This mode, one of the least effective ever devised by man, served well enough in an age that demanded only a specified fragment of each human being's whole abilities. There was, however, no warranty on the human products of mass education.

That age has passed. More swiftly than we can realize, we are moving into an era dazzlingly different. Fragmentation, specialization and sameness will be replaced by wholeness, diversity and, above all, a deep involvement.

Already, mechanized production lines are yielding to electronically controlled, computerized devices that are quite capable of producing any number of varying things out of the same material. Even today, most U.S. automobiles are, in a sense, custom-produced. Figuring all possible combinations of styles, options and colors available on a certain new family sports car, for example, a computer expert came up with 25 *million* different versions of it for a buyer. And that is only a beginning. When automated electronic production reaches full potential, it may be just about as cheap to turn out a million differing objects as a million exact duplicates. The only limits on production and consumption will be the human imagination.

Similarly, the new modes of instantaneous, long-distance communication—radio, telephone, television—are linking the world's people in a vast net of electric circuitry that creates a new depth and breadth of personal involvement in events and breaks down the old, traditional boundaries that made specialization possible.

The very technology that now cries out for a new mode of education creates means for getting it. But new educational devices, though important, are not so central to tomorrow's schooling as are new roles for student and teacher. Citizens of the future will find much less need for sameness of function or vision. To the contrary, they will be rewarded for diversity and originality. Therefore, any real or imagined need for standardized classroom presentation may rapidly fade; the very first casualty of the present-day school system may well be the whole business of teacher-led instruction as we now know it.

Tomorrow's educator will be able to set about the exciting task of creating a new kind of learning environment. Students will rove freely through this place of learning, be it contained in a room, a building, a cluster of buildings or an even larger schoolhouse. There will be no distinction between work and play in the new school, for the student will be totally involved. Responsibility for the effectiveness of learning will be shifted from student to teacher.

As it is now, the teacher has a ready-made audience. He is assured of a full house and a long run. Those students who don't like the show get flunking grades. If students are free to move anywhere they please, however, there is an entirely new situation, and the quality of the experience called education will change drastically. The educator then will naturally have a high stake in generating interest and involvement for his students.

To be involved means to be drawn in, to interact. To go on interacting, the student must *get somewhere.* In other words, the student and the learning environment (a person, a group of people, a book, a programmed course, an electronic learning console or whatever) must respond to each other in a pleasing and purposeful interplay. When a situation of involvement is set up, the student finds it hard to drag himself away.

The notion that free-roving students would loose chaos on a school comes only from thinking of education in the present mode—as *teaching* rather than *learning*—and from thinking of learning as something that goes on mostly in classrooms. A good example of education by free interaction with a responsive environment already exists, right before our eyes. Watch a child learn to talk or, for an even more striking case, watch a five-year-old learn a new language. If the child moves to a foreign country and is allowed to play intensely and freely with neighborhood children—*with no language "instruction" whatever*—he will learn the new tongue, accent-free, in two or three months. If instruction is attempted, however, the child is in trouble.

Imagine, if you will, what would happen if we set the five-year-old down in a classroom, allowed him to leave his seat only at prescribed times, presented only a few new words at a sitting, made him learn each group before going on to the next, drilled him on pronunciation, corrected his "mistakes," taught him grammar, gave him homework assignments, tested him and—worst of all—convinced him that the whole thing was work rather than play. In such a case, the child might learn the new language as slowly and painfully as do teenagers or adults. Should an adult try to learn a language by intense play and interaction, he would probably do much better than he would in a classroom, but still fall short of a young child's performance. Why? The adult has already learned the lessons that the old schooling teaches so well: inhibition, self-consciousness, categorization, rigidity and the deep conviction that learning is hard and painful work.

Indeed, the old education gives us a sure-fire prescription for creating dislike of any type of human activity, no matter how appealing it might seem. To stop children from reading comic books (which might be ill-advised), you would have only to assign and test them on their content every week.

Learning a new language is a giant feat, compared to which mastering most of the present school curriculum should prove relatively simple. All sorts of equipment eventually will be available for producing responsive environments in all the subject matter now commonly taught, and more. Programmed instruction, for example, creates high involvement, since it draws the student along in a sort of dialogue, letting him respond at frequent intervals. Programming at its best lets the student learn commonly agreed-upon cultural techniques and knowledge—reading, spelling, arithmetic, geography and the like—in his own time, at his own pace. But present-day programming may soon seem crude in light of current developments. Computers will be able to understand students' written or spoken responses. (Already they understand typed responses.) When these computers are hooked into learning consoles, the interplay between student and learning program can become even more intense.

When computers are properly used, in fact, they are almost certain to increase individual diversity. A worldwide network of computers will make all of mankind's factual knowledge available to students everywhere in a matter of minutes or seconds. Then the human brain will not have to serve as a repository of specific facts, and the uses of memory will change. In the new education, breaking the time-worn, rigid chains of memory may have greater priority than forging new links. New materials may be learned just as were the great myths of past cultures—as fully integrated systems that resonate on several levels and share the qualities of poetry and song.

Central school computers can also help keep track of students as they move freely from one activity to another, whenever moment-by-moment or year-by-year records of students' progress are needed. This will wipe out even the administrative justification for schedules and regular periods, with all their anti-educational effects, and will free teachers to get on with the real business of education. Even without computers, however, experimental schools are now finding that fixed schedules and restrictions on students' movements are artificial and unnecessary.

Television will aid students in exploring and interacting with a wide-ranging environment. It will, for example, let them see into the atom or out into space; visualize their own brainwaves; create artistic patterns of light and sound; become involved with unfamiliar old or new ways of living, feeling, perceiving; communicate with other learners, wherever in the world they may be.

Television will be used for involvement, for *two-way* communication, whether with other people or other environmental systems. It will most certainly not be used to present conventional lectures, to imitate the old classroom. That lectures frequently do appear on educational television points up mankind's common practice of driving pell-mell into the future with eyes fixed firmly on the rear-view mirror. The content of each brand-new medium thus far has often been the ordinary stuff of the past environment.

The student of the future will truly be an explorer, a researcher, a huntsman who ranges through the new educational world of electric circuitry and heightened human interaction just as the tribal huntsman ranged the wilds. Children, even little children, working alone or in groups, will seek their own solutions to problems that perhaps have never been solved or even conceived as problems. It is necessary here to distinguish this exploratory activity from that of the old "discovery method," championed by some theorists, which is simply a way of leading children around to standard perceptions and approved solutions.

Future educators will value, not fear, fresh approaches, new solutions. Among their first tasks, in fact may be *un*-learning the old, unacknowledged taboos on true originality. After that, they may well pick up a new driving style in which they glance into the rearview mirror when guidance from the past is needed but spend far more time looking forward into the unfamiliar, untested country of the present and future.

In a sense, the mass-produced student of the present and past always turned out to be a commodity—replaceable, expendable. The new student who makes his own educational space, his own curriculum and even develops many of his own learning methods will be unique, irreplaceable.

What will motivate the new student? Wide variations between individuals will make competition as we now know it irrelevant and, indeed, impossible. Unstandardized life will not provide the narrow measures needed for tight competition, and schools will find it not only unnecessary but nearly impossible to give ordinary tests or grades. Motivation will come from accomplishment itself; no one has to be forced to play. Form and discipline will spring from the very nature of the matter being explored, just as it does in artistic creation. If the student of the future may be compared with the child at play, he also resembles the artist at work.

A strange dilemma seems to arise: it appears that, with the new modes of learning, all the stuff of present-day education can be mastered much more quickly and easily than ever before. Right now, good programmed instruction is cutting the time for learning certain basic material by one-half or one-third. What will students do with all the time that is going to be gained? The problem is not a real one. With students constantly researching and exploring, each discovery will open up a new area for study. There is no limit on learning.

We are only beginning to realize what a tiny slice of human possibilities we now educate. In fragmenting all of existence, Western civilization hit upon one aspect, the literate and rational, to develop at the expense of the rest. Along with this went a lopsided development of one of the senses, the visual. Such personal and sensory specialization was useful in a mechanical age, but is fast becoming outmoded. Education will be more concerned with training the senses and perceptions than with stuffing brains. And this will be at no loss for the "intellect." Studies show a high correlation between sensory, bodily development—now largely neglected—and intelligence.

Already school experimenters are teaching written composition with tape recorders (just as students play with these marvelous devices) in an attempt to retrain the auditory sense, to recapture the neglected rhythms of speech. Already experimental institutes are working out new ways to educate people's neglected capacities to relate, to feel, to sense, to create. Future schoolings may well move into many unexplored domains of human existence.

Can we view this future, the hard and fast of it? Never, for it will always come around a corner we never noticed, take us by surprise. But studying the future helps us toward understanding the present. And the present offers us glimpses, just glimpses: seven-year-olds (the slowest of them) sitting at electronic consoles finishing off, at their own pace, all they'll ever need in the basic skills of reading, writing and the like; eight-year-olds playing games that teach what we might call math or logic in terms of, say, music and the sense of touch; nine-year-olds joining together in large plastic tents to build environments that give one the *experience* of living in the Stone Age or in a spaceship or in an even more exotic place—say, nineteenth-century America; ten-year-olds interacting with five-year-olds, showing them the basics (now unknown) of human relations or of the relationships between physical movements and mental states.

In all of this, the school—that is, an institution of learning confined to a building or buildings—can continue to hold a central position only if it changes fast enough to keep pace with the seemingly inevitable changes in the outside world. The school experience can well become so rich and compelling that there will be no dropouts, only determined drop-ins. Even so, the walls between school and world will continue to blur.

Already it is becoming clear that the main "work" of the future will be education, that people will not so much earn a living as learn a living. Close to 30 million people in the U.S. are now pursuing some form of adult education, and the number shoots skyward. Industry and the military, as well as the arts and sciences, are beginning to consider education their main business.

The university is fast becoming not an isolated bastion but an integral part of the community. Eventually nearly every member of a community may be drawn into its affairs. Already, though not many journalists or college presidents realize it, the biggest news of our times is coming from research in the institutions of higher learning—new scientific discoveries, new ways of putting together the webs of past and current history, new means for apprehending and enjoying the stuff of sensory input, of interpersonal relations, of involvement with all of life.

The world communications net, the all-involving linkage of electric circuitry, will grow and become more sensitive. It will also develop new modes of feedback so that communication can become dialogue instead of monologue. It will breach the wall between "in" and "out" of school. It will join all people everywhere. When this has happened, we may at last realize that our place of learning is the world itself, the entire planet we live on. The little red schoolhouse is already well on its way toward becoming the little round schoolhouse.

Someday, all of us will spend our lives in our own school, the world. And education—in the sense of learning to love, to grow, to change—can become not the woeful preparation for some job that makes us less than we could be, but the very essence, the joyful whole of existence itself.

BEYOND CAMPUS CHAOS

TROUBLED by ugly images of campus riots, the American citizen may have two perfectly reasonable questions: "Why the protests?" and "What can be done to stop them?" The standard answers rarely are clear. The "issues" run all over the map—free speech, the war, war work, the draft, ROTC, the construction of a gymnasium, admissions policy, black studies, coeducation, dormitory visiting hours. Experts often dissect these issues as if they were separate and compelling in themselves. Others, seeking comfort in simplicity, argue that all the protesting students are caught up in a "Communist conspiracy." Still others, quoting the most militant students' own words back at them, blame a pure cussedness, a rebellion with neither cause nor goal.

When it comes to stopping the trouble, most people think first of direct repression. University administrators debate tactics; news magazines list them in neat categories (choose your own). Legislators in California, epicenter of the uproar, have proposed over 100 new laws to put the protesters in their place, which, according to many of the laws, would be jail. Some lawmakers feel that campuses should be fenced in or surrounded by high walls. Anyone wishing to get in or out would have to present identification to guards at the gates. Thus the business of education could proceed.

All of this fails the best tests of logic and utility. We need a far deeper response to "Why the protests?" than talk about the now-familiar "issues" (though almost all of them are important). If every individual grievance were remedied next week, there would still be turmoil on our campuses next fall.

Higher education is in agony because it is shockingly outmoded. Its inability to anticipate and comprehend—much less deal with—the needs of black students is only one measure of its obsolescence. The agony of the colleges will begin to end when all concerned cease merely *reacting* to individual crises. Take the typical U.S. college trustee. He is white, Protestant, nearing sixty, politically conservative and quite likely a businessman. He is probably willing (for whatever motives) to make all sorts of changes in his business while insisting that the school under his trusteeship remain essentially the same. Perhaps the trustee is a banker. Today, his once-staid institution leans heavily on electronics, hard-sells loans and savings, floods the mails with credit cards and hires female tellers for their coiffures and sex appeal. Not even the sternest old values have escaped the revolution in banking. In fact, if the Thrift once preached as a cardinal virtue were now practiced, our national economy would collapse.

That any college policy maker can fail to push, and push hard, for basic reform in college education is not just disgraceful, it is insane. The fact of the matter is, higher education *will* change. It will change in a constructive manner, with the help of all concerned, or violently, against mindless resistance. Violence is certainly not necessary, but swift and drastic action probably is. Start with some modest proposals:

1. *Admissions.* Present-day admissions policies are nothing less than a travesty on education. They assure that a minimum of learning (individual human change) will take place between graduation from high school and graduation from college. The "best" universities admit only those students who already can score high on verbal-rational tests. The students continue scoring well on such tests or are dropped. "The university can then point with pride," educator Harold Taylor writes in his book *Students Without Teachers,* "to the fact that its undergraduate curriculum is so good that 40 or 50 percent of the freshmen are eliminated after the first year. From this it could be argued that the best institution is one so good that very few could be admitted and no one at all could graduate."

Those truly committed to education, to the full development of human possibilities, might argue for a different kind of "best" college, one that would admit the *bottom* ten percent of high-school graduates, then help them develop. But this may be extreme. Perhaps we should now ask only that the best colleges use not test scores, but a simple lottery to decide who gets in. This one stroke would end the present cultural bias as well as the expense of the admissions bureaucracy and the agony of students and parents seeking the mana of the élite school. What is more important, the college itself would have to change. Deprived of pretested students who are likely to pass exams in spite of inadequate teaching, it would be forced at last to learn something about learning.

2. *Courses, lectures, exams, grades.* Separate, competing courses fragment the student. Teachers vie to make up formidable assignments, scheming for their fair share of his effort. The student learns cunning. He asks himself not, "What can I learn?" but, "What do they want?" He attends regularly scheduled lectures, though experiments show that the most powerful learning rarely occurs on any fixed schedule. The lecture mode continues because of custom, because of administrative convenience, because of a belief in magic. My daughter, an honor student at Berkeley, boycotted her lectures in sympathy with a student strike during one winter quarter. Unburdened of classes, she read avidly, discussed what she read with friends and family. She turned in her papers and took her final exams. Her grades were revealed to be slightly higher than they had been the previous quarter. Her case was not exceptional.

Every term, every day, more and more students and teachers are awakening from the sleep of their senses. Teachers make assignments against the threat of exams and call it "teaching." The hoax wears thin. Assign-and-test is not teaching. Routine lectures are rarely more than a fairly innocuous form of white magic. And when a student suddenly opens his eyes and cries, "The emperor has no clothes," hundreds of thousands more who have already made the discovery are there to echo him.

At the least, we can propose that the undergraduate program revolve around coherent student projects rather than courses and exams. And we can hope that college educators, in cooperation with students, will get on with the task of creating learning environments in which the tools and resources of learning will be available *all the time,* wherever possible. Technology can help. Electronic and mechanical learning devices, like books, are always ready and tireless. For some kinds of learning, they may surpass books by giving the learner responses as he goes along. Even without new technology, we can devise an environment that avoids the tyranny and inefficiency of fixed scheduling and mass instruction. In pursuit of relevant projects, students can learn by themselves or with others, on campus and off. Faculty members can spend most of their teaching time simply being available for individual help and for those informal discussions that so often generate an excitement foreign to the formal lecture.

Grades are the glue that holds an obsolete contraption called "college" together. The arguments pro and con grading are familiar. We need only say here that the justification for grades finally comes down to the fact that *somebody else* along the line needs them. The student certainly does not. He probably needs more precise and more relevant feedback than letter or number grades can give him. He needs frank comment from his teachers and from fellow learners. He needs guidance in developing his ability to learn joyfully, for any other kind of learning is ultimately inferior and self-defeating.

3. *Buildings.* "American universities are spending about five billion dollars annually to build campuses that are disfunctional in many ways for their present inhabitants, and almost certainly will be obsolete in the near future." After making this statement in a government-sponsored research paper, the noted American architect Sim Van der Ryn adds, "The university environment as it comes off the assembly line is most often an Edsel." Van der Ryn feels

that five billion dollars a year is not too much, only wrongly spent. That it isn't too much is open to question. In any case, every new building designed for conventional classrooms or massive lecture halls adds one more obstacle to educational reform, and therefore contributes to the continuation of campus violence.

Indeed, if some of the present Edsel-like college buildings can't be totally remodeled, it might better serve education if they were donated to the community or dismantled. This would help force higher education out into the home and the community, where it could find new vitality and a new destiny. Recent campus strikes and boycotts, whatever the immediate outcome, have had one side effect that will be felt for years to come: teachers who have met with their students off campus, in their own homes or elsewhere, have generally experienced an intensity of learning unknown in the formal classroom setting. Now many teachers, striking or not, are seeking ways to take learning off the campus. A professor of political science at a Southwestern state university told me what happened when his class met at a student's swimming pool: "Skeptics might say it was just a party—and it was. But look what happened. In class, we meet for 50 minutes. Discussions tend to get formal and routine. At the pool, we talked about political science for two and a half hours nonstop; then some students in small groups went on with the discussion into the evening. From this and other experiences, I've just about concluded that not only ordinary classrooms but ordinary clothes put distance between people and hinder learning. Maybe the best possible place for learning is the swimming pool." Those who would reject this idea out of hand might try it first.

What kind of buildings *could* be useful on the campus today? Architect Van der Ryn says it as well as anyone:

> A campus designed for learning would be a different place. Instead of massive lecture rooms, there would be videotape libraries and individual viewing stations on campus or at home. Instead of rows of identical classrooms, there would be many smaller places for groups to meet informally, adjacent to their laboratories, libraries, homes, offices, and workshops. The "classroom" is where teachers are and where learning takes place. The "classroom" is where you find it.

4. *War work.* If U.S. colleges and universities want to stay in touch with the best of the new generation of students—and end campus violence—they will simply have to renounce all connections with military research and development. War work is an inappropriate and corrupting activity for an institution of higher education. Other institutions can examine their own consciences.

5. *Curriculum.* Today's curriculum cheats the student by splitting off thought from action, mind from body, intellect from feeling. Educators who insist that higher education must be limited to the cultivation of the "mind" bear responsibility for making college irrelevant to the real world. Indeed, our "intellectual standards" are too low precisely because certain academicians have made "the life of the mind" stereotyped, repetitive, narrow and divorced from reality. We do violence to the intellect by severing it from the world of the senses. We do violence to our thoughts by separating them from their consequences.

Take the traditional liberal-arts curriculum. It promises, through reading, discussing, listening to lectures about and taking exams on certain great classics, to create a cultivated, honorable man. And it is true that in classical literature we can explore many of the root questions of human existence—freedom and authority, peace and war, human waste and human potential. But the liberal-arts curriculum has failed to use this material effectively. Young men have read the words, joined the discussions, heard the lectures and given the right answers on the exams. Then they, like others less "educated," have gone out into the world and furthered unjust wars, exploited natural and human resources, defrauded their competitors and their government, engaged in ruinous love affairs and marriages, and reared neglected, miserable children. As now presented, the liberal-arts curriculum is an exercise in compartmentalization, teaching the ultimate irresponsibility: that words and acts live in separate worlds.

It is not that we don't need Plato. We need Plato made whole. To make him whole, we must place him in a context larger than just words, a context of feelings, actions and consequences. The curriculum must include work or social action by the student in his own *polis,* his own community, however he may define it. Plato, in *The Republic,* warned against the study of philosophy by the uncommitted and the unexperienced. To teach Plato in a vacuum of consequences is merely trivial. If higher education is to be consequential, a student must have a chance to practice the art of putting thought and action together. The test of this education will be not a student's ability to verbalize, but the way he lives.

The time is overdue for the liberal-arts curriculum (and other curricula as well) to include what Aldous Huxley called the "nonverbal humanities"—the arts of better sensing, perceiving, feeling and relating with others. Such "subjects" already are offered by private institutes, experimental colleges and free universities. They can rejuvenate traditional curricula and keep new material from becoming irrelevant at birth. If the emerging departments of black studies, for example, resort to the old teaching (limited to reading assignments, lectures and exams), they are likely to become as stilted and inconsequential as some departments of white studies are. Methods as powerful as those of black-white confrontation currently are available to make the black experience an emotional as well as verbal reality, and to rescue it from academic interment. Simply to teach—and live—with absolute openness and honesty can revolutionize the campus and the society without violence.

Even in conventional "subject matter" terms, most U.S. college curricula are dangerously out of date. Philosopher Michael Scriven of the University of California at Berkeley argues that "the magnitude of the mismatch between our education and our needs has been grossly underestimated by even the 'extremist' critics." He proposes an "education for survival" curriculum that would prepare students in a very practical sense for survival in a technological world of constant change. Scriven would replace much of conventional literature with science fiction; he would teach the workings and ethics of government and the like by sharing power on the campuses; he would accord as much intellectual status to the skilled auto mechanic as to the physician.

Still, the colleges and universities, in any attempt at relevance and survival, will have to reexamine the whole question of tutoring the professions. As it is now, they tend to serve as glorified trade schools for industries and agencies that could do much of the training better, and at their own cost. Universities might also consider getting out of the certification business, passing this responsibility along to the professional organizations themselves, relieving the degree pressure. Thus higher education would become less expensive, less cumbersome and more relevant to the central matter of developing citizens capable of a lifetime of learning.

The modest proposals offered above suggest others, equally important. Streamlining administrations, getting a strong student and faculty representation on governing boards, and ending the tyranny and exclusivity of academic departments come immediately to mind.

Opponents of reform carelessly cite a "silent majority" as a measure of opposition to student protest. But the key word in the phrase is "silent." The silence measures higher education's essential dullness, its failure to inspire commitment.

Our college of the future should not be dull. Nor will it be built on a single, fixed plan. It will appear in many forms, to meet varying individual needs. Pluralism itself becomes a chief characteristic of any useful new learning. We need *many* positive plans for higher education. Student protesters are criticized for their lack of positive proposals. The same criticism weighs even more heavily on the older generation. Since World War II, the chief mode of thinking and writing about our society has been analytic and negative. The moment has arrived for our best thinkers to come out from the safety of their critical battlements onto the field of affirmations. By imagining better ways of doing things, we do not lock ourselves into rigid "positions," but we do establish the psychic preconditions for constructive reform. Every student and educator, every reader, is invited to envisage a college of the future. Here, in outline, is the beginning of one vision:

1. *Open Learning.* In our college of the future, all the learning environments physically located on the campus will be kept open 24 hours a day where possible. This includes libraries, laboratories, learning consoles, tape and film centers, dance and rehearsal halls, gymnasiums, and places for student discussion and encounter. The facilities can be staffed, and paid for, on a demand-and-use basis. (Like most reforms proposed here, this makes for increased efficiency and economy.) Faculty members will simply post the hours they are available for learning consultation, on campus or off. Certain events—special lectures, theatrical presentations and the like—may have to be scheduled, but, again, will be open to all on the basis of supply and demand. This means that learners can make their own learning schedules. The open system bridges the gap between student and nonstudent.

There would be many "degrees" of "student." Some would live at home, others, on campus, and still others, in self-supporting work-and-learn communes. The open system also will prevent that familiar moment of frustration when, just as an idea or a project takes fire, somebody has to put you out and shut a door.

2. *Research.* To share the perils, disappointments and joys of the scholar's quest is to enter a learning environ-

ment of great power. Research projects in our college of the future ought to be available as learning aids to far more than just graduate specialists, not after they are neatly wrapped up in scholarly journals, but *in process.* Search and discovery should certainly flourish. Since there will be little of the usual routine classroom teaching, the customary conflicts between research and learning will not exist. The two, properly conceived and practiced, inscribe an unbroken circle.

3. *Communication.* The media of communication—radio, television, film, the stage, the gallery, the light-sound show and the like—are particularly well adapted to the new learning. They can be used to spread that learning throughout the community. Beyond this, our college of the future will have a high stake in new, multipurpose communications devices. Home consoles can serve as television receivers and as learning machines as well. Their keyboards will be hooked into a central university computer that could have dialogues with home learners. These devices can also print out copies of material transmitted electronically from the university library. Every home becomes a "classroom." And the whole community is the university. Then, too, as all the world's learning centers are joined in a single communications network, the power of education will expand dramatically. We do not have to wait for futuristic electronics to begin this joining.

4. *Ceremony.* College has always had a certain ritualistic function. Formal celebrations, fraternity initiations, the ecstasies of Saturday afternoon have, in their own ways, marked the passage of youth. But these ceremonies have

gone stale and are inappropriate to this age. Our college of the future will have a unique opportunity to create new rites of passage. During these events, the learner can explore his relationship with nature; with other races, the opposite sex and the older generation; with campus authority and the spiritual realm; and, finally, with his own mind and body. These events are not abstract. To confront the natural world, for example, students in small groups go out into the wilderness for extended periods. A student may also move through a series of 24-hour marathon confrontations. Of late, our society has provided few things people are willing to stay up all night for. It is certainly worth this effort for the gut-level experience of what it is like to be of another race, another sex or another generation. Racial encounter, for instance, might continue at intervals all year long or until understanding is reached. The ceremonies may be climaxed by a private vigil and perhaps a fast, during which the student comes to grips with his most formidable adversary: himself. There will be celebrations, too, festivals to replace the stilted graduations we have known. From all this comes substance and savor that give meaning to the "life of the mind." Classical literature will take on new dimensions for students who have deeply experienced the basic concerns of our time.

But this is just a beginning. Some students have assumed that the new education will be "easy," that once grades, exams and the like are removed, everything will be solved. This is not true. The new education demands far more energy and commitment from every learner and educator. The student radical had better realize that, when he asks for the committed life, he is putting himself on the line. And people of every age and calling must know that educational reform implies real reform in our social order and its values. The way to peace, on the campus as well as in the world, is toward creative change. Every banker, every college president, every teacher and student feels in his bones that change is coming. All can join in transforming our colleges, now.

PART IV

MEN, WOMEN AND A FUTURE

SOME people still believe that "problems" can be "solved." They assume that each difficulty can be defined and isolated, studied by experts, then assigned to specialists and technicians who will manipulate the appropriate variables and wrap the matter up. The key assumption here is that the experts, specialists and technicians can *act upon* things and people while remaining fixed in their own behavior and being, much as a hydraulic press shapes metal. Certain problems, it's true, still submit to this classic Western mode of solution. When men can agree on a specific technological goal (a nuclear device, men on the moon), they may get results without ostensibly troubling their own ways of feeling and acting and believing. Even this is open to question.

In any case, the major difficulties of our age—violence, racial strife, ecological rape, overpopulation—are not easily *acted upon*. Humane men of medicine drastically reduce death rates in "backward" areas, and create poverty, famine, strife and a tendency toward dictatorship. Progressive agronomists drastically increase crop yield per acre, and poison the life of the air and the sea. By the fruits of their own works, specialized experts have disqualified themselves. The fragmenting boundaries they have so jealously guarded now crumble in the flood of a new reality.

The West developed its externalized problem-solving mode in times of expansion, empire and the frontier. That mode required space for wasting as well as resources for exploiting. The debris of each "solution"—human as well as material—was simply cast aside as the frontier marched ahead, *acting upon* man and the world. But now actions turn back upon themselves. We are confronted with the consequences of our creations; the fall of a sparrow does signal our destiny. The "race problem" is not something "out there" that we can fix or hire an expert to fix. We must change ourselves. Getting in or out of wars like Vietnam has less to do with logistics than with sex.

All matters, it turns out, are interrelated. And no matter is more central than our concept and feelings about what it means to be a man or a woman. For example, the pride, aggression, hot competitiveness and desire for dominance summed up by the Mexicans as *machismo* contributes very directly to militarism and violence, racism, overpopulation and the rape of the planet. It may be, in fact, that no new politics is possible without a new sexuality.

Perhaps it is provocative to suggest that statesmen, scientists, administrators and technicians bent upon influencing outside events look first at their own relationships with lovers and friends, wives and children. If so, let that be my chief provocation. For today every "solution" is personal, dwelling not entirely "inside" (as some humanistic psychologists now claim) nor entirely "outside" (as most managers and technicians have long assumed), but in the interaction of the two. To change the world, start with both.

THE FUTURE OF SEX*

IN TODAY'S most technologically advanced societies, especially urban Britain and America, members of the younger generation are making it clear—in dress and music, deeds and words—just how unequivocally they reject their elders' sexual world. It is tempting to treat the extremes as fads; perhaps many of them are. But beneath the external symptoms, deep transforming forces are at work.

Sex as we now think of it may soon be dead. Sexual concepts, ideals and practices already are being altered almost beyond recognition. Marriage and the family are shifting into new dimensions. What it will mean to be boy or girl, man or woman, husband or wife, male or female may come as one of the great surprises the future holds for us.

We study the future the better to understand a present that will not stand still for inspection. Today, corporations, foundations and governments are asking a new breed of experts called "futurists" to tell them how things are going to be. These futurists tend to limit their predictions to things rather than people. Their imaginations and their computers fight future wars, knit future systems of economics, transportation and communication, build future

* With Marshall McLuhan.

cities of fantastic cast. Into these wars, systems and cities, they place people just like us—and thereby falsify all their predictions. By default rather than design, most futurists assume that "human nature" will hold firm. They ignore the fact that technological change has always struck human life right at the heart, changing people just as it changes things.

This may be especially true of sex. A history of mankind in terms of sexual practices would make wildly variegated reading. Many ancient civilizations, for example, encouraged varying degrees of incest, and the Ptolemies, successors to Alexander the Great, practiced marriage between brother and sister for some 300 years with no obvious ill effect. Modern anthropologists have brought back stories of present-day primitive tribes whose sex customs confound our traditional notion that there is only one "natural" pattern of relationship between the sexes.

In early man, just as in most of the higher mammals, males and females lived rather similar lives, with little specialization except where childbearing and childrearing were concerned. Life for every member of a primitive hunting tribe was integral, all-involving; there could be no feminist movement, nor any special class of homosexuals or prostitutes. But when mankind turned from hunting to farming, and then to creating cities, empires, pyramids and temples, men and women were split apart in ways that went far beyond biology. Many men became specialists—kings, workers, merchants, warriors, farmers, scribes—in the increasingly complex social machine. Most women fell heir to less specialized, but separate, domestic tasks.

With the coming of writing, it was the manly virtues that were recorded and extolled. As Charles W. Ferguson points out in *The Male Attitude,* men have kept the records of the race, which may explain why history is a chronicle of war, conquest, politics, hot competition and abstract reasoning. "What survives in the broad account of the days before the modern era," Ferguson writes, "is a picture of a humankind full of hostility and inevitable hate." (Until relatively recent times, female births and deaths often were not even recorded.) Ancient writers exaggerated the biological as well as the social differences between the sexes, with the female coming off very badly indeed.

The Romans invented the word *sexus,* probably deriving it from the Latin verb *secare,* "to cut or sever." And that is exactly what civilization has done to man and woman. The cutting apart of the sexes rarely has been more drastic than in the industrial age of Europe and America, the period that was presaged by the invention of printing around 1460 and that is now changing into something new right before our eyes.

Throughout the Middle Ages, there had been less separateness between men and women. Privacy, for example, was unwished. Houses had no hallways; bedrooms served as passageways and sleeping places for children, relatives and visitors, along with married couples. Under such circumstances, the sexual act merged easily with the rest of life. Language now considered intimate or vulgar was part of ordinary conversation. Childhood did not exist as a separate category. At about age seven, children simply moved into the grown-up world; paintings of that day depict the young as scaled-down adults, even to the matter of clothing.

After printing, however, human life became increasingly compartmentalized. Architecture took up the idea of visual enclosure, with private rooms connected by hallways. It was only when this happened that childhood separated out from the rest of life. At the same time, sexual activity went underground. Hidden and mysterious, it receded into a realm apart from ordinary existence, becoming more and more fraught with a special intensity, a vague anxiety. Indecency, pornography and obscenity came into being as a result of specialist stress on separate parts of the body. By the time of Queen Victoria, the split between sex and the proper life was complete. Any wedding night, after a five- to ten-year engagement, was likely to be a trauma.

Freud flushed sex up out of the underground, but he, like his contemporaries, saw it as an explosive, a possible threat to whatever held civilization together. In his time—and even up to the present—the forces of life seemed constantly at odds with one another; since the Renaissance, it has seemed necessary to pen them up in separate compartments. The industrial age built more than its share of these boxes. It split class from class, job from job, profession from profession, work from play; divorced the self from the reality and joy of the present moment; fragmented the senses from the emotions, from the intellect; and, perhaps most importantly of all, created highly specialized and standardized males and females.

The ideal male of the industrial age was "all man." He was aggressive, competitive, logical. This man of action was also an apostle of the abstract. And he feared to show much emotion. The ideal woman, for her part, was emotional, intuitive, guilefully practical, submissive. Maleness and femaleness were separate territories; man and woman shared only a tiny plot of common humanity. The wonder is that the two could get together long enough to continue the race.

When sex—under the influence of Freud, factories, the automobile and world wars—came out into the open to become SEX, a peculiar thing happened: people were *supposed* to be free and frequent with their sexual activity; women were *supposed* to turn from Victorian propriety to passionate responsiveness. And yet the basic ideals of maleness and femaleness continued unchanged. It was like a revolution without popular support: a lot of slogans, shouting and confusion, but not much revolution.

The only real attempt at change up until the present turned out to be abortive. Women of feminist persuasion, viewing the action and the power over there in the arena of aggressiveness, specialization and hot competition, tried to take on the attributes of maleness. They may have been heading in the wrong direction. When the Victorian novelist George Meredith wrote, "I expect that Woman will be the last thing civilized by Man," he was unknowingly describing her fitness for the *post*civilized age. Where the old technology split people and the world apart, demanded human fragmentation, the emerging technology is putting Humpty Dumpty back together again. It is most doubtful, in the new age, that the rigidly "male" qualities will be of much use. In fact, there may well be little need for standardized males *or* females.

Trying to define a new sexuality in the industrial period, D. H. Lawrence placed his characters against a backdrop of factories, mines, smokestacks. His most successful sexual hero (in *Lady Chatterley's Lover*) was a gamekeeper; he may be viewed as the closest Lawrence could get to the primitive hunter. In a sense, the man of the future will be a hunter, an adventurer, a researcher—not a cog in a social machine. The coming age, linked by all-involving, instantaneous, responsive, electronic communication, may seem more "tribal" than "industrial." The whole business of sex may become again, as in the tribal state, play—freer, *but less important.*

When survey takers "prove" that there is no sexual revolution among our young people by showing the frequency of sexual intercourse has not greatly increased, they are missing the point completely. Indeed, the frequency of intercourse may *decrease* in the future *because* of a real revolution in attitudes toward, feelings about and uses of sex, especially concerning the roles of male and female. What are those young men with long, flowing hair really saying? In what may seem a ludicrous overstatement, they are sending a clear message to all who will listen: "We are no longer afraid to display what *you* may call 'feminine.' We are willing to reveal that we have feelings, weaknesses, tenderness—that we are human. And, by the way, we just may be ridiculing all of those up-tight movie males with cropped hair and unflinching eyes. We're betting they can't touch our girls." Indeed, the long-haired boys' appeal is not esthetic, but sexual; not private, but corporate.

Bear in mind that the Beatles' dazzling early success, long before their remarkable musicianship came clear, was conferred upon them by millions of young *females* who were transported by those page-boy hairdos and those sensitive faces. And the Beatles were not the first in a modern lineage of girl-movers. A younger, slenderer, tenderer Frank Sinatra and then a hip-swiveling Elvis Presley had reduced earlier subgenerations to squeals and moans. It takes a particularly obstinate blindness not to realize that an ability to free emotions, and not a fragmented "all-maleness," provides today's most compelling erotic appeal.

We might also confess that our reading of the new teen-age "conformity" of dress and hairdo fails to consider the social ritualism of these forms. They express the new desire for depth involvement in social life rather than egotistic eccentricity.

The trend (perhaps without the exaggerated hairstyle) seems likely to continue. The all-sensory, all-pervasive total environment of the future may be no place for the narrow-gauge, specialized male. Emotional range and psychic mobility may be valued. Heightened intuition may be required. The breed of hombre generally portrayed by John Wayne is already an anachronism. "Be a man!" the hombre bellows, and the more perceptive of our young laugh.

And if the narrow-gauge male is not laughed out of existence, he may, literally, *die* out. Specialized, competitive man is particularly susceptible to the maladies of the involuntary-muscle, nervous and vascular systems. A U.S. male's life expectancy now is seven years less than a female's. Figures on earlier times are impossible to verify, but one thing is sure: the gap has never been greater. Men who operate inside the boxes of fragmented civilization—whether bus driver, production-line worker or professional specialist—die off at an alarming rate from the heart and gut diseases. Figures for the peptic ulcer are particularly revealing: deaths for white men are four times that for white women in the U.S. But the female death rate, as women have started pushing into the man's world, has been rising. And what about today's younger generation, those under twenty-five? Here are the children of TV and science fiction, the pioneers of the electric age, the first humans to sample, even briefly and incompletely, the less fragmented, less competitive, more involving future. What of these tentatively retribalized young men? We may predict that their ulcer rate will decline.

No surprise. In the most isolated primitive tribes, those whose members still operate as free-roving hunters, digestive disorders are practically unknown and the usual civilized heart troubles are rare. Significantly, these people make little distinction between the ideal qualities of male and female. As the noted British anthropologist Geoffrey Gorer writes concerning the peace-loving Pygmies of Africa, the Arapesh of New Guinea and the Lepchas of Sikkim:

> Men and women have different primary sexual characteristics—a source of endless merriment as well as more concrete satisfactions—and some different skills and aptitudes. No child, however, grows up with the injunctions, "All real men do . . ." or "No proper woman does . . . ," so that there is no confusion of sexual identity: no cases of sexual inversion have been reported among them. The model for the growing child is one of concrete performance and frank enjoyment, not of metaphysical, symbolic achievements or of ordeals to be surmounted. They do not have heroes or martyrs to emulate or cowards or traitors to despise; . . . a happy, hardworking and productive life is within the reach of all.

It would seem that "being a man" in the usual, aggressive Western sense is, if nothing else, unhealthy. To live an ordinary peacetime life in the U.S.—as an Army study of the "nervous secretions" of combat soldiers in Vietnam shows—is as bad or worse for your gut, heart and nervous system as facing enemy bullets. But the present fragmented civilization seems on its way out, and what "being a man" means could swiftly change.

Extremes create opposite extremes. The specialized, narrow-gauge male of the industrial age produced—in ideal, at least—the specialized woman. The age stressed the visual over the other senses; the fast development of photography, and then movies, helped pull femaleness up from the context of life, of actuality, and make it something special, intense, "hot."

Grotesque and distorted extremes tend to pop out just at the end of any era, a good example being the recent rash of blown-up photographic nudes. The foldout playmate in *Playboy* magazine—she of outsize breast and buttocks, pictured in sharp detail—signals the death throes of a departing age. Already she is beginning to appear quaint, not sexy. She might still be possible for a while in a wide-screen, color movie (another hot medium). But try to imagine her, in that same artificial pose, on the intimate, involving television set in your living room.

Don't throw away your *Playboy* foldouts, however. Sooner than it may seem possible, those playmate-size nudes may become fashionable as collectors' items, having the same old-timey quality for future generations that cigar-store Indians and Victorian cartoons have for us. This is not to say that nudity is on its way out. On the contrary, it will most likely increase in the neo-tribal future. But it will merge into the context of ordinary living, becoming not so much lurid and sexy as natural and sensuous.

It is toward a common humanity that both sexes now tend. As artificial, socially imposed distinctions disappear, the unalterable essentials of maleness and femaleness may assume their rightful importance and delight. The lusty Gallic salute, *Vive la différence!*, rings truer about biology than about mores, mannerisms and dress. Even fashion speaks. "Glamour" was a form of armor, designed to insulate, to separate. The new styles, male and female, invite dialogue.

While both sexes will probably change, most men will have farther to go than most women in adjusting to the new life. In an unspecialized world of computers and all-enveloping communications, sensitive intuition and openness will win more prizes, if you will, than unfeeling simplistic logic. Right now, it is impossible to guess how many companies are being held together by intuitive and sensitive executive secretaries. Fortunate is the enterprise that has a womanly woman (not a brittle, feminist dame) as a high-level officer. Many forward-looking corporations, especially in the aerospace industry, already are engaged in sensitivity-training sessions for their male executives. The behavior encouraged in these sessions would make a John Wayne character wince: manly males learn how to reveal their emotions, to become sensitive to others, to weep openly if that is what they feel like doing—all this in the pursuit of higher profits. Sensitivity *works.* The new technology—complex, interrelated, responsive—demands it.

The demands for new male and female ideals and actions are all around us, changing people in many a subtle and unsuspected way. But there is one specific product of modern technology, the contraceptive pill, that can blow the old boundaries sky high. It makes it possible for sexual woman to act like sexual man. Just as the Bomb instantly wipes out all the separating boundaries essential to conventional war, the Pill erases the old sexual boundaries in a flash. The Pill makes woman a Bomb. She creates a new kind of fragmentation, separating sexual intercourse from procreation. She also explodes old barriers between the sexes, bringing them closer together. Watch for traditions to fall.

Romantic Love seems a likely victim. As a specialty, romance was an invention of the late Middle Ages, a triumph of highly individualistic enterprise. It requires separation, unfulfillment. The chase is everything—the man aflame, the maiden coy. Sexual consummation bursts the balloon of yearning. As in the romantic movies, the significant embrace can hardly be imagined without "The End" printed over it. Indeed, what we have called sex in recent decades may be viewed as the lag end of Romantic Love.

As a way of selecting a spouse, romance ("In all the world, you are the only girl for me") never worked very well. Back in the eighteenth century, Boswell may have felt some shock at Dr. Johnson's answer to his question: "Pray, Sir, do you not suppose there are fifty women in the world, with any one of whom a man may be as happy, as with any one woman in particular?" Johnson replied: "Aye, fifty thousand." The future may well agree with Dr. Johnson. It is difficult to play the coy maiden on a daily diet of contraceptive pills. And the appeal of computer dating suggests that young people are seeking out a wide and quite practical range of qualities in their mates—not just romance or high-intensity sex appeal. Here, in fact, may be the electronic counterpart of arranged marriage.

The great mystics have always perceived Romantic Love as somehow defective, as a double ego that selfishly ignores other people. Today's youngsters have a different way of putting it: "Our parents' generation is hung up about sex."

As Romantic Love fades, so may sexual privacy. Already young people shock their elders by casually conversing on matters previously considered top secret. Hippies and post-hippies have reverted—boys and girls together, along with a few little children—to the communal living of the Middle Ages or the primitive tribe. It is not uncommon to find a goodly mixture of them sleeping in one room. Readers who envisage wild orgies just don't get the picture. Most of the hippies are *not* hung up on sex. To them, sex is merely one of many sensory experiences. It is available when desired—therefore perhaps not so desperately pursued.

Today sex is returning to the adult world just as childhood is once again becoming enmeshed in grown-up matters. The dream girl or dream guy is becoming as odd an idea as the dream house in a world of integral urban design. Sex is becoming secondary to the young. At the same rate that it becomes accessible, it is cooling down. A couple of teenagers like Romeo and Juliet would now have some of their most dramatic moments deciding on the kind of education they want for their children, plus a second career for Romeo in middle age.

In future generations, it seems most likely that sex will merge with the rest of life, that it will settle down and take its place within a whole spectrum of experiences. You might not think so, what with the outpouring of sexed-up novels and plays since World War II. But these, like the slickly pictured playmates, bring to mind the death rattle of an era. The more that modern writers present sexual activity as a separate, highly defined, "hot" aspect of life, the more they hasten the death of SEX. Most "literary" novelists have not yet discovered the present, much less glimpsed the future; which is one reason that so many of the brighter college students have turned to antinovels and, in spite of its questionable literary reputation, science fiction. Robert Heinlein's *Stranger in a Strange Land,* a popular underground book, tells of an attempt to set up Martian, rather than the usual human, relationships here on earth. In these relationships, what we term sex is communal and multisensual. There is no sharp, artificial distinction between male and female roles. Sex blends with other activities that might be called mystical. And there is even the need for a new word (Heinlein calls it "growing closer") for this demi-erotic mode of relating. Many young people see something of their own aspirations in the Heinlein book and others similar to it. Norman O. Brown (*Life Against Death, Love's Body*) strikes an equally sympathetic response with his thesis that civilized man has even fragmented his physical person. According to Brown, many people can feel sexual pleasure only in the sex organs themselves; the rich sensory universe of the rest of the body has been deadened.

Just as the electric age, with its multitudinous communication aids, is extending the human nervous system *outside* the body, it is also creating a new desire for exploration inside the self. This inner trip seeks ways to awaken *all* the senses, to find long-lost human capacities, to discover turn-ons beyond the narrowly sexual. One instance of this new drive for depth involvement is the growing national interest in Oriental religion and philosophy; another, riskier, one is the increasing use of LSD and marijuana among young people. These drugs, the experimentalists claim, very quickly "blow your mind," which is to say, they knock out the old partitions within the self, allowing new connections to be made. Some theorists also say that rock music with psychedelic light effects can aid the inner traveler.

Serious researchers are looking for means of accomplishing even more without the use of drugs. In several centers throughout the U.S., they are working out techniques for awakening the body and senses, especially those other than the purely visual, and for helping people achieve the unusual psychic states described, for example, in the literature of mysticism. The future will likely demonstrate that *every* human being has capacities for pleasure and fulfillment beyond sex that the present barely hints at.

In this rich context, those reports on the death of the American family may turn out to have been premature. Actually the family may be moving into a Golden Age. With so much experiment possible, marriage may come later in life than ever before. Future family units may not be separated from each other in little capsules, but may join together in loosely organized "tribes." As it is now, the capsular family often has nowhere to turn for advice and encouragement when in need, except to professional counselors or organizations. The informal tribe of the future can provide a sounding board and a source of support for each of its families, far more responsive and loving than any professional helper.

With marriage coming later in life, it may also become a more serious matter—perhaps as serious as divorce. Some couples may even wish to write up a legally binding separation agreement (to be revised when their financial and parental situation changes) as a precondition to marriage. Thus, in a sense, marriage becomes "divorce." With all this unpleasant business anticipated and accomplished even before the nuptial vows are spoken, divorce becomes far easier—and probably far less likely. In any case, the divorce rate will probably fall.

Marriage—firmly and willfully welded, centered on creative parenthood—may become the future's most stable institution. The old, largely discredited "togetherness" was based on stereotyped concepts of each family member's role. The new family, integral and deeply involving, may provide the ideal unit for personal discovery, for experiment in the seemingly infinite possibilities of being human. Each new child can provide a new set of perceptions for all the family. Each develops rapidly, urges change in parents and other children alike. It is possible that the family of the future may find its stability in constant change, in the encouragement of what is unique in each of its members; that marriage, freed from the compulsions and restrictions surrounding high-intensity SEX, can become far more *sensual,* that is to say, more integral.

What about homosexuality and prostitution? Lifelong, specialized sexual inversion has baffled many researchers. But may it not be viewed simply as a response to sexual overspecialization? Just as men in our society are far more specialized than women, so male homosexuality is far more prevalent. To "be a man" in the narrow sense has often proven difficult and dehumanizing. In certain stressful and ambiguous family situations, some young men have not been able to pull it off. So they flip-flop over to the coin's reverse side, the mirror image of hypermaleness—even more specialized, even more limiting. If a new, less specialized maleness emerges, it is possible that the need to turn to specialized homosexuality will decrease. There is a striking absence of it among the communal-living young people of today.

As for prostitution, if it is the oldest profession (or, if you will, service industry), it is also one of the most ancient specialties—an early consequence of the creation of man-in-the-mass. Armies, merchant fleets, work forces: men without women demanded Woman, or at least one aspect of her. So long as men are massed and shipped away from home, this female specialist will likely follow. But, like homosexuality, prostitution may also be looked upon as a response to a certain kind of hyperfemaleness. When men, as in the Victorian Age and long after, require sexually inhibited wives, they create an equal and opposite demand for sexually uninhibited partners-for-pay. As the first requirement fades, so does the second. Already call girls are becoming game for the aging. The whole notion seems somewhat ridiculous to the young.

Indeed, the future may well wonder why there has been so much fuss about sex over all these years. Sex may well be regaining some of its traditional cool. It is still a three-letter word, despite the efforts of its four-letter relatives to hot it up. This is not to say the future will be sexless. Far from it, generations yet to come may very well find *all of life* far more erotic than now seems possible.

Those who try to puzzle out any *single* sexual way for the next age will probably find their efforts in vain. Rather, it seems, the future holds out variety and diversity. The search for a new sexuality is, after all, a search for a new selfhood, a new way of relating. This search already is well under way. What it turns up will surprise us all.

THE MAN & WOMAN THING

WE CAN ORBIT the earth, touch the moon. Visions of feathery cities in space no longer outrage our sense of the possible. And yet, this society has not devised a way (though love propels our very existence) for man and woman to live together for seven straight days with any assurance of harmony and personal growth. No wonder. The spacemen spend billions on communications, billions more on research and development. They build and fit with exquisite care. They renounce sleep and comfort for their mission's sake.

How different it is with marriage today. Few couples have any training whatever in communicating true emotions, which carry the kind of information needed to make a marriage fly. The space age has spawned no major research-and-development program on the man & woman thing. Unlike a missile, a marriage generally is conceived and constructed in a slapdash, hit-or-miss fashion. And rare is the man who would devote to his domestic affairs even a fraction of the time, talent and energy he gives his "work."

We dedicate ourselves to job, school, politics, golf. We let love take care of itself. What happens? A joining that begins in passion relapses into cliché while the first fresh taste of love is still on your lips. The moment comes (too soon!) when you run across tax forms among old love letters. "Notice Of Adjustment. Part I—Tax-Payer's Copy." And suddenly, Sunday finds you sprawled not on that high, singing meadow where the eyes of your love were able somehow to hold the universe but in front of the TV. After six hours of pro football, the most brilliantly executed fake buck and roll-out seems trivial; the beer tastes like used detergent; the peanuts lie like hot mud at the bottom of your belly. Your love walks by, and a mechanical hand (one of yours?) reaches up to pat her on the fanny. As for her, she shakes her head and moves to check the washing machine. The machine churns in the background. Everything is secure. But your love isn't there. Her mind has flown her to that faraway sea of poppies on the edge of the cornfield where she is saying over and over, as did Madame Bovary, "O God, O God, why did I get married?"

Yes, marriage for most is only a scrap of what it could be. The dismal figures on divorce need no further viewing-with-alarm here. And when experts estimate that marital problems cause a yearly loss of billion and a half dollars in industry, they barely hint at the deeper sickness. Marriage experts William J. Lederer and Dr. Don D. Jackson state that a "stable-satisfactory" marriage is "almost hypothetical." "We have never observed," they write, "a generally constant collaborative union between spouses during the period when they are raising children." What seems worst, in fact—the couple in tumultuous combat—often is really best. And what seems best—the couple locked in deadly contentment—may be worst. Of the latter, Lederer and Jackson write:

> In a quiet, socially respectable manner the people in this group suffer more pain, hate more profoundly, and cause more discomfort to others than do the members of the other . . . groups. *Yet the spouses appear to be unaware of their behavior.* There is a deadly virulent glue of hate that is only visible to the keen eye of the behavioral scientist or the brilliant novelist.

Marriage has provided, among other things, a convenient mechanism for maintaining the physical, emotional and sexual status quo for both partners, blocking personal growth. When a couple is "made for each other," this can simply mean that their neuroses mesh. But if our perceptions of the American marriage have never been darker, its prospects may never have been brighter. Marriage could provide an ideal setting for personal development. It could open a way to lifelong learning. It could encourage the evolution of new social forms, a matter of more importance than moon shots. Such a marriage—a new man-and-woman thing—is the subject of this search.

Start with the question of dedication. A handsome California family may serve as our point of departure. We'll call them the Dawes. Joe and Ginny Dawes, their three children and their new baby almost mock the all-American ideal, so snugly do they appear to fit it. Joe is a former football star and Marine officer; Ginny, a former beauty queen. They live an hour's drive from San Francisco in a neat little suburban house-with-pool. The children excel in sports and make top grades. They go to church. They know how to laugh about what they are doing.

But the Dawes are different from most people in their

circumstances: they burn with an uncommon devotion to their family. They work at it, to the point, if necessary, of sacrificing money and social status.

This commitment was what drew photographer Paul Fusco and me to them. We knew plenty of "successful" men who used their home and family merely as psychic service stations. Mr. America, it seemed to us (and what with deadlines and travel assignments, we could afford no smugness), is a visitor to his home, and his "success" in the world generally is measured by the shortness of his visits.

How many of those cover stories have you read in the newsmagazines? Formal and predictable, they sing of Mr. Executive, who has transformed Omnipex Electronics from a penny-ante gadget shop to a corporate entity intent on gobbling its competitive way around half the globe. Or Mr. Statesman, who is ushered through a truly incredible day that begins at dawn with coffee and communiqués in bed, and ends, after the state dinner, with a "second day" at the office. About two-thirds into the story, you sense a slight shift in tone as a cardboard family is rolled onstage. There is a mercifully brief recounting of the idyllic courtship, the lean and loyal early years, the arrival of the heirs; and then the wife is allowed a sentence or two. Rueful but proud, she affirms her role as the humble handmaiden of Success, and drops out of sight as the story moves on to its justification-for-practically-anything: Manly Service to Others.

But another message squeezes up between the words: perhaps these corporate and public servants would do better to serve not "others" but themselves and their families. They rarely do anything to enrich our lives, because they have not enriched their own. And what can justify the unjelled, resentful children they loose like a plague on the world?

Let the newsmagazines have their hard-line homage to Success. We would seek heroes of marriage and the family.

So we found the Dawes—Joe, thirty-eight, Ginny, thirty-three, Joe, Jr., thirteen, Laura, twelve and Sharon, ten. We visited them during the weeks that led up to the birth of the fourth child: picnics, homework, chores, a father-and-son project, a moment of closeness, a moment of apartness. The days go by. An unseen child thrusts and squirms in Ginny's womb. No hot news here. Look again. It is all as commonplace and as magical as falling leaves before the snow and springtime foliage after. Like your family. Like mine.

Because Ginny loves Joe with no conscious doubts, she is free to be womanly. She does not hide the fact that she enjoys the company of men. When you are with her, you are aware of all the feminine vibrations; yet it is possible to be comfortable and open, to be—really—friends. This rare man-woman relationship—so often spoiled by pseudo-seductiveness or pseudo-prissiness—grows only on a sturdy tree of love. Ginny can be a real woman *and* a friend.

But at times she turns inside herself. Then some of the light dims. No big dark cloud falls on her face, but a small, torn, wispy one. "She got married too young," Joe tells us. "It cut into her fun years. She was not quite nineteen. Ginny's a creative person. When the children are older, she may go out and do something. She feels confined at home."

The courtship and wedding, all moonlight and orange blossoms, might have been fashioned by Scott Fitzgerald. And yes, there were the lean and loyal early years: reality and tears in a rickety apartment near a Marine base in North Carolina; pro football with the 49ers; the insurance business in Southern California; three children perhaps too soon.

Here, we depart from the newsmagazines. In 1961, Joe made his decision to renounce glory and the buck: he would go back to college and get the M.A. in recreation he had always really wanted; his central commitment would be to his own family.

That commitment is strong and sometimes stern. It includes a rule of no adult guests (except family groups) on weekends, nothing to interfere with family outings, family games. When Ginny explained it to me, I inadvertently wrote her words in five lines that seem to make a miniature ode to her household:

Our family comes first
We help others as we can
We fall short sometimes
Loving each other
We're a very close family

By commitment alone, without recourse to experiment, relying on the oldest American values, the Dawes have achieved much, perhaps enough to confound the more pessimistic experts. But it would be unfair to push them up on a pedestal and burden them with gold medals inscribed "ideal." Even though Joe is not chasing personal fame or riches in his present job, he is still sometimes preoccupied with it. And Paul and I sensed a certain tension and stiffness between parents and children, due perhaps to a strong emphasis on everyone's putting forward a bright and shining face to the world and each other at all times. As in most American families, any expression of negative feelings—discouragement, resentment, anger, hurt—is frowned upon. Joe tells Joe, Jr., to trim the hedge. Joe, Jr., makes a face. *Snap.* "No football game." Joe, Jr., repents. He takes his anger out on the hedge. And that's all there is to it.

Don't blame the Dawes, however, for the national conspiracy to wrap life in pretty plastic. Our society manages to conceal much of what is real—death, birth, love, even parts of our history. And when reality threatens to show itself, the "professionals" are right there to keep it sanitized and out of sight. This is all very convenient, but it robs us of the richness and fullness of existence. Especially in the man & woman thing (as we'll see later), the conventional efforts to conceal, to deceive by omission can lead to tension, confusion and exhaustion.

When the birth of the Dawes' baby approached, Paul asked Ginny if he could photograph the entire process. He showed her earlier pictures he had taken of a birth. These lovely portraits reveal life's most awesome moment not through any kind of clinical detail but through the mother's face as she experiences pain and then tears of joy. Ginny liked the pictures and invited Paul to come along when the time arrived. She would certainly have him with her and Joe in the labor room. But she couldn't promise she'd let him into the delivery room; it would be according to how she felt at the time.

The baby was two weeks late. Paul went to the hospital with Joe and Ginny, and he photographed most of the labor. But at the end, Ginny made him leave. Waiting outside, he began thinking about the births of his own two children and how he, like Joe, had been excluded from the delivery room. This is what he wrote in his notebook:

Ginny Dawes is in labor. I sit on the front fender of a car outside her room. The mystery will be guarded. I feel the desire to go through this thing of birth again with my wife, together this time, with people who will understand that "yes, it is a mystery, but one to be seen and heard and rejoiced in."

It was only by accident that I witnessed a birth and saw pain lead to ecstasy and love, and only then did I feel anything real about what my wife had known about birth. Someday, births should be shown with sound and living color on local and national television all the time so that we can all once again understand and experience the mystery instead of just seeing a woman in pain being wheeled down a hallway away from you. How can we hope to understand anything about it when the professionals steal the moment and look at it as a clinical problem instead of looking into the eyes of the woman and feeling a joining of hands with God in giving forth life?

It won't be long now. It's been a long day for Ginny. I feel a need to go storming into the room, demanding to see it all, to photograph it, to display it before the nation and to say, "See. It exists. It's real." And we are all real. Everything we do is real. Everything we feel is real, and we don't have to hide emotions and tell others to lie about their feelings.

A while back, in the labor room, Ginny was in harder labor and Joe asked her if she wanted me to leave, even though I was not taking pictures any more, because, "We don't want to show anything that isn't nice." "Yes," Ginny said. "I'm at the point where I can't hide it now." Hide it? Why hide it? Let it out. Let it go where it wants to!

(Later) Well, she did it: 8 pounds, 12½ ounces. Pamela Jane. Just before the birth, standing in the hall outside the delivery room, Joe and I heard three long, loud, yelling grunts with intervals of silence in between. They were strange cries of deep victory. Then quiet. Before we expected it, the door swung open and there came Ginny, baby beside her, and she was RADIANT. She had had no drugs, barely a whiff of gas, and she did it alone. It showed! Pink, flushed face. Bright, shiny eyes. The baby was all red-faced and squinted under the bright lights in the hall. Joe was happy and relieved. He kissed Ginny and smiled at the baby, but it seemed to me he had been robbed of the deeper meaning of the experience. It remained the property of the professionals. And the lie prevailed, the lie that tells us life's most powerful emotions must be forever hidden.

But now Pamela Jane is out of the hospital and into the world we have built for her. No surgical mask will block her view of our faces, only the masks we learn to wear for hiding our hearts. We'll not peer at her through a nursery's plate-glass window, only through the unacknowledged barriers between our senses and reality. The Dawes will give Pamela Jane love and care and extraordinary attention. But she will rear *her* children in the twenty-first century. By then today's family relationships—however diligently crafted—may no longer work at all.

Beyond our best traditional efforts, beyond contentment, lie unexplored lands of love. In search of them, my wife and I participated in a week-long couples' workshop at Esalen Institute on the Big Sur coast of California with 17 other couples. A little later, Paul Fusco and I took notebook and cameras to a similar workshop that lasted four weeks. This encounter-group situation does not permit "observation" in the traditional sense; Paul and I became participants as well as observers.

What is the desired outcome? The workshops pursue something pretty far out: an intensified monogamy dedicated to honesty, loyalty and old-fashioned man-and-woman love. If a couple learns its lesson well, no thought or feeling will remain hidden. Even the most fleeting sexual fantasy will be revealed. Every petty resentment, every jealousy guarded tenderness will be laid on the line. The man-and-woman thing that comes of all of this—labeled the Open Couple by Dr. William Schutz, the leader of our workshop, and described as High Monogamy by a New York poet—has no clear historical precedent.

Here is how the workshop begins: the couples gather in a large, heavily carpeted room. There is no furniture; only a few scattered cushions. Heavy wooden latticework protects the glass that makes up one of the room's walls. Dr. Schutz, a bearded, bearlike man in his early forties, preludes the first meeting with a little talk on what kind of world we might have if openness, honesty and the sure, true revelation of feelings were the rule rather than the rare exception in business, politics, diplomacy—and in love, too. He tells of the outlandish amounts of energy used to maintain deceptions, energy that could better go into constructive activities. During the workshop, the couples would have opportunities to tear down the walls of deception and distrust not through polite talk but the most strenuous and consequential acts.

He starts with a few simple exercises. Participants practice the expression of feelings that are generally hushed up in polite society, pounding on the floor and roaring or screaming. They practice nonverbal communication by circulating around the room, getting to know other people by silently exploring faces with their hands. They find out how much they really trust their partners by taking turns falling backward into each other's arms. What becomes clear very quickly is the chasm between what people *say* about themselves and what they really *feel.*

Then the bombshell: Schutz asks all the participants to close their eyes for a few minutes and think of three secrets they have never told their partners. The secrets should be the kind which, if revealed, would seriously jeopardize the marriage. After about five minutes, Schutz suggests that everyone open his eyes. He asks quietly: "Now, who would like to reveal one of the secrets?"

Expressions of disbelief and apprehension flash around the room, then—surprisingly—a woman raises her hand. She is asked to bring her husband to the center of the room, to sit there and, looking him in the eyes, to tell the secret. This tense-faced woman with large features and a British accent could still be beautiful, but the corrosive years have eaten away at the corners of her mouth and eyes. As for the husband, his face is clenched as tight as a fist. The woman begins diffidently, but quickly is swept away by a torrent of words and tears. Ten years ago, she recounts, she fell in love with another man and asked for a divorce. She reminds her husband how he blocked it by terrifying legal threats. She, a foreigner new to this country, had not known her rights and had given in to the threats. Now she wanted him to know that she had spent the past decade as a bitter prisoner, motivated from day to day only by her hatred for him. Often, she said as he sat there silently, she had wished his death.

At the end of these revelations, something like a sigh rose in the room. What hope was there for this couple, especially after such a disclosure? Others followed, not always so spectacular but somehow deeper and more significant. Here were respectable, well-to-do couples, most of them "happily" married, reciting episodes and feelings that, by all rights, would destroy any marriage. But "confession" for its own sake was not the aim. This was only the beginning.

During the days that followed, the couples practiced a number of techniques for a closer marriage—fantasy or guided daydreams, sense-awareness training, psychodrama and the like. But the three secrets continued to provide the framework upon which everything was built and also to motivate spectacular learning experiences.

Here and now, I must strongly advise the reader against trying the three-secrets technique with his spouse alone or without an experienced leader. Deprived of the proper context, the experiences could be disastrous. The disclosures might strike up *argument* rather than *encounter*. "Encounter" means simply owning up to your own feelings and revealing your deepest here-and-now emotions, no matter how painful, how dangerous-seeming or how embarrassing. "Argument" means making points, passing judgments and handing out recriminations. Argument is generally repetitive and circular. It is "logical." And if there is one sure thing about marriage, it is that logical argument in a highly charged situation makes the least sense of all. In the encounter-group situation, the leader keeps things moving and also keeps things from getting out of control. The other couples give perhaps even more crucial help: they are quick to cut off circular arguments; they provide feedback at critical points, so that each couple can see itself clearly mirrored in the honest reactions of the others. The group also physically supports and comforts when that is needed.

* * *

How explosive the three secrets can be was shown by a rather quiet, well-mannered couple from the Midwest. Jack was an accountant; Eileen, a high-level executive secretary. They had four children. At first appearance, their marriage seemed mild enough, but as it turned out, each of them was harboring lies within lies within lies. And the effort to protect the lies was sapping much of the energy and even twisting the personality and physical appearance of each. Jack had a sort of blustery charm, but he could go straight from bluster to a kind of mushy sentimentality with no relevant behavior in between. Whenever the talk came anywhere close to the hidden areas in his life, his language and manner could become exceptionally pompous and confusing; he could neither understand what was being said to him nor was he to be understood. Eileen protected her falsity by becoming exhausted. When anything started closing in on her hidden life, her face would lock in a mask of weariness; her eyes would narrow to slits out of which pain and resentment glinted. In this state, she seemed unable to *hear* anything that threatened.

On the workshop's first full day, someone asked Jack if he ever played around. "No. Er—*no!*" he blustered. But his eyes blinked, he swallowed twice and reached for a cigarette. When the group broke up for "dyads" (one-to-one encounters) that afternoon, Eileen and I had a talk about Jack's reaction.

"I heard him swallow," she said. "I know he's not telling the truth." A little later, she muttered: "I'm not, either."

I asked her if she were planning to tell her secrets. She said *that* would be utterly impossible; it would surely shatter her marriage.

That night, in the group, Jack surprised her. They sat

in the middle of the floor. Tension had been building up in him all afternoon. He blurted out the facts and then the details of two extramarital affairs. Eileen's shock was apparent, but a few minutes of meaningless questioning passed before she was able to mobilize her feelings. Then she sprang for his throat. The couple rolled on the floor as she attacked and he fended her off. The other couples glanced at Schutz, wondering if he would stop the fight, or if they should. Schutz lounged, imperturbable, on an elbow. Having been in an earlier group with him, I knew how fast he could move when a fight threatened to become dangerous. I also knew he would let the battle resolve itself if possible. Schutz feels that outrages accumulate during the years of marriage, and that often the outrage can best be expressed by some form of physical violence. Now Eileen was ripping off Jack's shirt, tearing at his back. He hurled her to the carpet. She attacked again. They were both panting, pausing, looking at each other. And suddenly they were in each other's arms, sobbing.

A few minutes later, Jack was talking almost straight. Eileen's eyes were not just slits. In fact, there was a certain sparkle in them. And Jack was displaying his torn shirt to the group, holding it aloft as a banner of victory. But wait. Eileen and Jack had taken just the first step in a long journey. They still faced much pain: talking, feeling, more revelations in the group for both of them, more fighting, more loving, more understanding. And then, at the end of four weeks, they were—really—different people: softer, surer, but by no means cocky. Like all long voyagers, they had gained a certain maturity and wisdom. They were aware of the distance traveled and the distance yet to go.

In these groups, time does strange tricks. Two days may

seem a season, since a greater number of honest, intense human interactions can occur in an hour of encounter than in a year of "real life." Still, all of it is not difficult and taut; there are happy moments when insight comes through laughter.

Si and Margo seemed to have everything. He was a research mathematician at a large university. They had inherited money and owned a home with a pool on several acres of land. They loved their two young children. And yet Margo was dissatisfied. She wanted something that would justify her existence.

"Sometimes I wish I had a huge, complicated machine," she told the group. "It would be in one room of my house, and only *I* could make it work. It would have all sorts of wheels and gears and belts and pistons, and it would make this marvelous sound, and it would fill the *whole* room. When people would come to call, they would ask—you know how they *always* ask: 'What do you *do?*' And I would take them to the room, open the door and say, *'There.'* "

Margo's machine delighted the group, especially the housewives; they all wanted one for themselves. Later Si and Margo were in the process of making their marriage come alive for the group. As it turned out, Si was compulsively neat, while Margo was compulsively messy. The group leader for that morning was a woman named Betty Fuller, who, dressed in a flowered muumuu, radiated the size, beauty and presence of a Hawaiian princess. Miss Fuller suggested that they swap roles and act out their neatness and messiness. Si, playing the part of Margo, began strewing wads of tissue all over the room. Margo, as Si, followed after him, nagging and picking up the mess.

The arguments became louder. They were yelling at each other. They were having a fine time.

"Wait a minute!"

Someone in the group had an idea: "Margo, you've *got* your machine. You mess up. Si cleans up. The gears mesh perfectly. It makes a lot of noise. Keeping it going keeps you busy. Perfect!"

Such episodes showed us how neuroses could mesh, how almost every couple seemed to be, in this negative sense, "made for each other." Unfortunately the mechanism often was far more destructive than Si and Margo's. And keeping it going could be a heavy drain on a couple's energy. We were amazed to discover how much of marriage was devoted to the maintenance of behavior anyone would reasonably want to drop right away. But servicing the neuroses at least could give marriage a reason for continuing, thus contributing to marital—and social—stability.

We could not abide this cynical resignation. Surely there existed ways to make marriage a mechanism for change and growth, something that would challenge each partner to the heights of his or her ability. After all, marriage is potentially the most intense as well as intimate of human relationships, the only one that involves every human system—all that it means to be human. But we could see that changing a marriage wouldn't be easy. It would demand the skill, the dedication—the heroism, even—usually reserved for politics, war or such epic endeavors as the conquest of space. All these endeavors confront us with times of crisis during which we may transcend ourselves, become nine feet tall and emerge as *different people*. In a society that has come to seem pallid and stiff to many, the workshops create such crises for couples. There must be other ways, for every man-woman relationship contains within it the seeds of an epic.

The long days and nights of the encounter presented us with many boundaries to cross. Significantly, the most difficult did not entail fighting, screaming or revealing lust and hatred. Giving and accepting love—not carefully or grudgingly, but with all the heart—stood before us at last as the most formidable boundary of all. Love itself, involving commitment and the ultimate consequences, elicited the most resistance, the most fear. I am not referring here to Romantic Love, which is another thing. That fine careless rapture, that idealistic yearning which can be traced to an itch in the bloodstream, is not really a commitment; often it is an escape from commitment. It supplies life's grace notes, but should not be mistaken for the symphony. The greatest poets and dramatists, sniffing out its essential flaws, have almost always shown us their fictional romantic lovers as tragedy-bound. The mystics have lamented the selfishness of Romance and have perceived it as a foreclosure on the human potential. Falling in love is not trivial, but it is easy. The challenge comes in taking that first love and making it grow into something larger and richer and more varied.

At times during the workshop, couples were asked to stand in opposite corners of the room and shout the worst things they could think about each other, getting it all out in the open where it could be dealt with. That is hard, but affirming real love is even harder. One night a middle-aged unmarried couple fell into a pattern of self-deprecation. Both had been divorced. She had a son. They had been living together for three years. Both were terrified of marriage.

"We know ourselves," she said mournfully. "We're B-minus people. We're with each other because no one else would have us."

I objected: "I'm sick of this. There's a lot that's beautiful about this relationship and about both of you. Why don't you get in opposite corners and shout the *best* thing you can think of about each other? Why don't you say, 'I love you because—'?"

Hesitantly they went to their corners. They looked at each other with dread. Finally he began: "I love the way you smile."

"Louder!" someone shouted. "If you mean it, say it like you mean it."

"I love the way you took care of Davy when he was hurt." Their voices grew stronger. Their declarations came faster, became more intimate, urgent. And then tears, signaling release and joy. They had been playing it safe. *Neither of them had known.*

These two were "engaged" during the four-week workshop, were married a few weeks later.

None of this should be read as a testimonial for High Monogamy. According to Schutz, only about 80 couples thus far have dedicated themselves to complete openness through his workshops—and this has been over the past 18 months. During this short period, a great deal of success has been reported. Who knows what will happen over the long haul? For one thing, giving up all concealment and deception doesn't *require* absolute fidelity in a New Testament sense; but for all practical purposes, it makes it inevitable.

Some people need—or think they need—the titillation of minor conspiracy, if not more.

The new openness would certainly destroy much of what we now call drama. It has spoiled every movie I have seen since my first workshop. In each of these, the entire plot has hinged on flaws in communication between men and women. The most elementary application of open encounter would have cleared up the situation in the first five minutes and made the rest of the movie unnecessary. This is a point of no small importance. Much of the resistance to deep-down change in human behavior comes from entrenched members of the Literary Culture, as well as from those who fabricate "suspense" in movies and TV shows. These men have a vested interest in the status quo; they find attempts to alter our ways of relating upsetting—even "embarrassing"—perhaps because they feel such basic human changes would make them obsolete.

But drama will not end when deception and confusion do. It will only *change*. Throughout most of our civilization, tragedy has been considered the most exalted form of art. But now futurists predict a turn toward something akin to high comedy, or even the creation of new "myths." J. R. R. Tolkien has written of stories that begin in joy and end in joy. Somewhere within these stories, as in fairy tales, there is a sudden turn, a "good catastrophe." "However wild its events," Tolkien wrote, "however fantastic or terrible the adventures, it can give to child or man that hears it, when the 'turn' comes, a catch of the breath, a beat and lifting of the heart, near to (or indeed accompanied by) tears, as keen as that given by any form of literary art."

Some of this quality enters into the quest for new marital space. The prudent writer here retreats into poetry or silence. There is no common journalistic language that adequately describes crossing a boundary into an unfamiliar territory of love. The dangerous moment of crossing is the moment of learning, the moment when the dragon suddenly turns into a beautiful princess. Strange things become familiar; familiar things, strange; and the most ordinary objects and events shimmer in the mythic light you previously had somehow failed to perceive.

Other voyagers explore a different kind of man-and-woman thing. They seek redefinitions of the family itself. Like brave family experimenters of earlier times, they question the assumption that one man plus one woman adds up to the ideal relationship. Paul Fusco and I looked in on several of these experiments. One was a hippie-style ranch "family" consisting of 27 adults and 13 children, in which each adult had his own room, and sex was "strictly up to the individual." Another was a family that started with nine middle-class adults who originally planned to share living quarters, money, children and sex. Another was a more modest arrangement of two families who had joined together to share everything *but* sex.

Perhaps by coincidence, most of these family experiments that shared bed partners broke up during the four months of our coverage. They had started with idealistic pronouncements, but, again, there was a wide gap between words and true motivations; the intelligent woman who theorized about "broadening the community of concern" really wanted, as it turned out, more sex. These exotic families seemed to suffer the same defects as the most ordinary couple. The man-and-woman thing that fails for two can fail even more disastrously for a dozen. And yet most experts agree on the need to end the isolation visited upon the tight little family in its tight little house or apartment.

Dr. Richard Farson, a co-founder of the Western Behavioral Sciences Institute, has proposed that married couples form networks to monitor each others' marriages and give honest feedback on how they can be improved. As it is now, his research has shown, the Browns can plainly see what needs to be done to improve the Joneses' marriage. And the Joneses can evaluate the Browns' as easily and accurately. But neither couple, under the present mode of relating, dares tell the other. Farson's network would encourage openness and encounter. It could serve as the foundation for a vast experiment to increase, among other things, the enjoyment of life.

And what can we do to make marriage a bit more "serious"—as serious as divorce, for example? Experts are increasingly attracted to the idea of "two-stage marriage." The first stage would be something like present-day engagement, except that the couple would enjoy society's approval for living together. It would be easy to get into and out of. No children could come of this gentle wedlock. The second stage would be reserved for those more mature couples who plan to stay married for life. This joining could include the conception and rearing of children. The second stage of marriage would be a most solemn matter, difficult to get into and out of. One of the best things about such a plan is that it would channel the energy of youthful love and sexuality into the approved institutions of society —rather than having this energy slip away into the underground.

Indeed, increasing the interaction between the couple

and the society might well be a chief goal in any movement toward a better man-and-woman thing. Concentrating on your marriage doesn't mean being preoccupied with it to the exclusion of the pressing problems of the outside world. We need a balance between in-turning and out-reaching. The close couple that turns outward successfully tends toward success within the marriage. The couple that works best within the marriage has more energy to devote to the urgent works of our time.

We might ask, at last: "Does the man-and-woman thing *have* a future?" The question may not be hypothetical much longer. Within ten years, scientists tell us, we may be able to choose the sex of our offspring. And experimenters already are working on ways to reproduce living organisms without mating male and female cells. This means it will someday be possible to have a world with only one sex, woman, and thereby avoid the squabbles, confusions and heartaches that have dogged this whole business of sex down the centuries. A manless world suggests several science-fiction scenarios. The most pessimistic would have society changing not at all, but continuing on its manly ways of eager acquisition, hot competition and mindless aggression. In which case, half the women would become "men" and go right on getting ulcers, shouting, "Charge!" and pinning medals on each other.

Even if we could, though, we'd not likely give up the man-and-woman thing. "Two" is a very round, very magic number, and it seems to be just about the right number of sexes. We can go a long way with what we have. In planning our brave voyaging, however, we'd better not yet picture a gleaming spacecraft poised for orbit. Let us evoke instead Kitty Hawk, a windy day, a frail craft made of wire and fabric. This man-and-woman thing dreams of soaring, but doesn't mind running up and down the beach for a few glorious moments aloft. It's a beginning.